25

GAME-CHANGING

PHRASES

THAT MAKES LIFE

EASIER

The Keys To Happy and Stress Free Living

Jordan Welsh

LitBooks

Publishing

GRAHAM

Table of Contents

INTRODUCTION

Words, as we know them, are seemingly simple configurations of letters, but within these configurations lie the immense power of creation, transformation, and emotion. Like the softest of murmurs that can start an avalanche or the tiniest ripple that heralds a wave, words are our world's most formidable tool, yet their depth and significance often go unnoticed. Each word, each sentence, is akin to a brushstroke on the canvas of life. While some sentences soar through our minds without much thought, others nestle deep within our souls, guiding our actions, beliefs, and values.

This book explores 25 such sentences; so profound, they possess the power to change our worldview, bring comfort in distress, and inject clarity in confusion. They're not just words, they're lifelines. And as we delve into their stories, we realize the ubiquity and wisdom they bring to our existence.

In this book, captivating and enlightening stories are shared to further explain each sentence and morals to go with. Be prepared to witness deep revelations; as this book unfolds like an intricately woven tapestry.

By the end, it's not just about those 25 sentences; it's about countless moments, numerous emotions, and infinite thoughts that resonate, linger, and inspire. Through these tales, we hope to remind you of the power that lies within you, the power to choose, to express, to heal, and most importantly, to live. Because, eventually, it's not just about saying these sentences but about embodying them, letting them soak your entire being and fill you up with hope, clarity, and purpose.

Welcome to the 25 sentences that makes life easier!

Chapter 1: Navigating Personal Emotions

Imagine you're steering a boat through a dense fog. Sounds a bit scary, right? That boat, in many ways, is like our heart and the fog, well, it's the whirlwind of emotions we feel. Sometimes, it's thick with joy, other times with sadness, and occasionally, it's an unpredictable mix.

Alright, so how do we navigate?

1. **Recognizing the Weather (Your Feelings):** First, you've got to know what you're sailing into. Is it happiness? Grief? Anger? Just like you'd check the weather before setting sail, it's essential to acknowledge and name what you're feeling. "Ahoy! I see you, frustration," or "Hello there, happiness."

2. **Keep A Trusty Map (Self-awareness):** Remember those old treasure maps in pirate stories? In this journey, self-awareness is your map. It's about knowing where you've been emotionally, understanding where you are, and having a hunch about where you might go next. It's saying, "Oh, I've been here before, and last time, a deep breath and a walk helped."

3. **Talk to the Seagulls (Share and Vent):** You know, seagulls, those noisy birds at sea? Think of them as friends or family. Sometimes, just chatting with them, or in this case, talking about how you feel, can be surprisingly helpful. They

don't necessarily need to offer solutions—just a listening ear or a knowing nod.

4. **Adjust Your Sails (Adapting):** Sometimes, the winds of emotion can be overwhelming. Instead of letting them topple your boat, adjust your sails. Find coping mechanisms: perhaps it's music, maybe it's journaling, or possibly it's a bit of chocolate and a good movie. The key? Adjust, adapt, and keep sailing.

5. **Anchor Down (Take Breaks):** It's okay to drop anchor and take a break when the emotional seas get too stormy. It's not running away; it's smart sailing. Give yourself permission to pause, rest, and then decide when you're ready to sail again.

6. **Remember, Every Sailor Has Stories (You're not Alone):** Lastly, every sailor has tales of storms and calm seas. Similarly, everyone faces emotional tides. So, next time you feel adrift, remember you're not alone. There's a whole community of sailors, just like you, navigating their feelings.

In essence? Navigating personal emotions is much like being a sailor. Some days the sea is calm, others it's stormy, but with the right tools and a bit of perseverance, we can all learn to sail smoothly. Below are stories that talks more on navigating our emotions and ways to go about it remembering that every journey, even the emotional ones, adds to our story.

1.1 Embracing Choices: "I still decide who annoys me"

There's an innate power to this statement, a reclamation of one's own sovereignty over emotions and reactions. In a world bustling with varying frequencies of opinions, judgments, and natter, this sentence is a subtle yet potent reminder: We are the conductors of our own symphonies, the captains of our souls' vessels.

Have you ever stood by the sea and noticed how some waves crash with fury while others merely kiss the shore? Life's annoyances are those waves, and our reactions, the shore. We decide which wave gets to crash and which gets to merely pass by. While the external world may never cease its relentless onslaught of noise, cacophonies, and unsolicited opinions, within our minds is a sanctuary. A place where we have the final say on who gets an audience and who doesn't.

"I still decide who annoys me" isn't just a sentence; it's a declaration of emotional independence. It's the comforting mantra whispered in moments of overwhelming discord. It's the gentle reminder that, even in the thick of chaos, our peace is ours to command.

In this chapter, as we dive into the tale of the overbearing neighbor and the serene wisdom of Mrs. Anderson, let us remember: Just as a discerning curator handpicks masterpieces for a gallery, so too can we curate our emotional landscape, choosing which influences to embrace and which to set aside. The power, always, is in our hands.

The Tale of the Overbearing Neighbor

Once upon a time in the heart of a busy city stood a quaint, somewhat weathered apartment building named The Maple Residences. Nestled among the towering giants of modern architecture, The Maple held stories of many souls, and among them was Mrs. Emily Anderson.

Ah, Mrs. Anderson! A kind soul with a penchant for sunflowers, she had this innate gift to see the silver lining, even in the most persistent of rainclouds. Every morning, without fail, she would greet the world with a warm cup of tea and gaze out of her window, absorbing the cacophony of life outside.

Enter Mr. Higgins. If The Maple Residences was a stage, Mr. Higgins fancied himself the unsolicited director. With a magnifying glass perpetually at hand, he didn't hesitate to peer into the lives of the residents, offering unsought advice, free critiques, and an abundance of opinions. If there was a cat stuck up a tree, Higgins knew. If Mrs. Sharma on the third floor had a disagreement with her daughter, Higgins was the first to "console" her—with an "I told you so."

Now, our dear Mrs. Anderson and Mr. Higgins were neighbors. Imagine, if you will, a symphony. Mrs. Anderson's life was the gentle flute, peaceful and rhythmic, while Mr. Higgins? The blaring trumpet, enthusiastic and, often, off-key. Every day, he'd share tidbits about someone's life or offer critiques on Emily's choice of curtains, plants, or even tea brands.

Most would fume. Some would retaliate. But Mrs. Anderson? She had an armor—her perspective. Instead of seeing Higgins as a nuisance, she saw him as a daily challenge, a puzzle of patience. She'd often chuckle, "I still decide who annoys me." And true to her word, she did.

She had her tactics, of course. When Higgins would begin his monologue about the new couple in 5B, Mrs. Anderson would gleefully ask him about the rare birds he spotted that week. Instantly, the conversation would veer towards his birdwatching passion, leaving no room for gossip.

And on days he commented on her window plants, she'd smile, "Oh, Mr. Higgins, I knew you'd notice! They're a new variety. I got them for bees. You know, saving the planet and all. But I'm thinking of adding roses next. What's your favorite flower?" Suddenly, the discussion wasn't about her choices but about nature's beauty.

Through Mrs. Anderson, The Maple Residences learned a lesson in patience, tact, and the art of mastering one's reactions. She showed them that you couldn't control the world's noise, but you can certainly choose what resonates.

The tale of the overbearing neighbor is not just about nosy neighbors or sunflower-loving ladies. It's a testament to the power we have within us—to choose our battles, our reactions, and our peace.

Remember, it's not the loudest notes that make a melody memorable, but the spaces in between, the pauses, and how they are used. Mrs. Anderson was a maestro of those spaces. And her message? Clear and beautiful: "I still decide who annoys me."

Lessons

From "The Tale of the Overbearing Neighbor," we can extract several invaluable lessons:

1. **The Power of Choice**: Regardless of external circumstances or individuals, we have the agency to choose our reactions. Mrs. Anderson's mantra, "I still decide who annoys me," epitomizes the essence of personal empowerment.

2. **The Art of Redirection**: Instead of confronting issues head-on, sometimes it's wise to redirect

conversations or situations. Mrs. Anderson skillfully shifted Mr. Higgins' focus from gossip to his passion for birdwatching or a shared love for flowers.

3. **Seeking the Positive**: Mrs. Anderson chose to see Mr. Higgins as a challenge rather than an annoyance, a perspective that transformed potential confrontations into opportunities for growth and amusement.

4. **Embracing Patience**: Instead of retaliating or expressing her annoyance, Mrs. Anderson exhibited patience, showcasing its power in maintaining peace and harmony.

5. **Active Listening**: Mrs. Anderson's strategy of discussing Mr. Higgins' interests and passions emphasizes the importance of active listening. By genuinely engaging with him, she steered conversations in constructive directions.

6. **Mastering One's Emotions**: Emotional intelligence, as portrayed by Mrs. Anderson, is an essential skill. Recognizing, understanding, and managing our emotions leads to more fulfilling interactions and a serene life.

7. **The Significance of Silence**: The story emphasizes not only what is spoken but also what is left unsaid.

The spaces, pauses, and moments of restraint can be just as powerful as words.

8. **Community Influence**: One individual's approach or attitude can impact an entire community. Mrs. Anderson's methods subtly educated her neighbors in The Maple Residences on patience, understanding, and perspective.

9. **Valuing Individuality**: While it's easy to stereotype or label someone based on their behavior, the story reminds us of the depth and multifaceted nature of individuals. Behind Mr. Higgins' gossipy exterior lay a passionate birdwatcher.

10. **Embracing Life's Melodies**: Just as in music, life isn't about the loudest moments but about the composition as a whole. The combination of highs, lows, silences, and crescendos creates a harmonious existence.

Each of these lessons serves as a reminder of the intricate dance of human interactions and the choices we make daily. Mrs. Anderson's tale is a beautiful ode to the idea that life isn't about waiting for the storm to pass, but about learning to dance in the rain

1.2 Prioritizing self: "I'm not doing this against you, I'm doing this for me"

In the grand mosaic of life, amidst the myriad colors of relationships, commitments, and responsibilities, there lies a singular, often overshadowed piece: the Self. You see, in our noble endeavors to be there for others, to fill roles, and to meet expectations, we often forget one essential truth. That being there for oneself isn't selfish; it's vital.

Picture this: a mother, let's call her Lisa, has always been the anchor for her family. She's there for soccer games, dance recitals, dinner preparations, even the pesky plumbing issues. Lisa's life was a swirling kaleidoscope of others' needs. Then one day, amidst the chaos, she felt an itch. An itch to paint. Something she loved, cherished, but had shelved away. Now, enrolling in a painting class meant she'd miss those soccer games or dance recitals occasionally.

And so, when she voiced this desire, she met with perplexed faces. "But mom, you'll miss my game!" her son exclaimed. With a gentle smile, Lisa responded, "I'm not doing this against you, I'm doing this for me." It wasn't about depriving her son of her presence, but about nourishing a part of her soul that had been dormant.

You see, life is somewhat like an airplane emergency. We're always told to put on our oxygen masks first before assisting others. Why? Because only when we're breathing can we effectively help those around us.

The phrase "I'm not doing this against you, I'm doing this for me" captures the essence of this wisdom. It's not about negating or dismissing others' feelings or needs. It's about acknowledging our own. It's an assertion, a declaration of one's importance in their own life.

For those naysayers who say it's selfish, remember this: a candle can't light others if it's burnt out. Prioritizing self isn't about diminishing one's love for others but about ensuring there's enough light, enough energy, to keep the love burning bright.

In a world that often feels like a tightrope walk, balancing commitments, and personal desires can be challenging. But every now and then, taking that detour, choosing that painting class, or simply saying no is essential. Not as a rebellion against others, but as a salute to oneself.

For in the end, as we stand before the mirror of time, it's crucial to recognize the person staring back. Not just as someone's parent, partner, or friend but as an individual. Vibrant. Whole. And worthy of their own time, love, and understanding.

Story of Maria's Sacrifices

Maria was no stranger to the ticking of a clock. Life in her quaint suburban town was marked not by grand events, but by routines. Mornings began with the soft hum of the mixer, as she blended her husband's favorite smoothie, and the gentle screeches of lunchboxes being opened and closed, signaling the start of her children's day.

"Mom, where are my blue socks?" her son, Jamie, would frequently ask.

"In the second drawer, beside the green ones!" she'd shout back while simultaneously flipping pancakes and answering an email from her boss.

Despite the frenzied mornings, there was a certain rhythm to Maria's life—a predictable cadence, where love and duty danced in harmonious steps.

It wasn't until one evening, during a rare quiet moment, that Maria stumbled upon an old shoebox filled with photos and trinkets from her past. Amongst the sea of memories, she found a photograph of a younger Maria standing atop a hill, hair wild from the wind, eyes bright with dreams. It was taken during her backpacking trip through Europe—a time when she had no plan other than to explore, learn, and be.

As the evening sun cast a golden hue on the photo, a sharp contrast emerged between the carefree girl in the picture and the woman she had become.

"Don't get me wrong," Maria mused aloud to herself, "I love my life. But somewhere along the way, did I become more of a service to others and less of a person?"

Months rolled on, but that thought persisted. It whispered in her ear during the PTA meetings, nudged her at dinner times, and echoed during late-night laundry sessions. And then, a flyer about a local art class caught her eye. A childhood passion she'd set aside for adulthood responsibilities.

"I think I want to join this class," she told her husband one evening, showing him the flyer.

"But who'll manage the kids and house? Isn't it too much with your job?" he asked, genuine concern evident in his voice.

And that's when Maria uttered the sentence that would redefine her path: "I'm not doing this against you, I'm doing this for me."

She didn't want accolades or grand gestures. All she desired was a few hours a week where she could be Maria the artist, not Maria the mom, the wife, or the efficient employee.

The first day of the art class was a revelation. With every brushstroke, Maria was reconnecting with a part of herself she thought she'd lost. The class became her sanctuary—a place where time stood still, and she was the composer of her world.

Of course, the house wasn't always spick-and-span, and occasionally, takeout replaced home-cooked meals. But what was previously seen as chaos now signified balance—a life where Maria could pour love into her family without draining herself.

In this journey of self-reclamation, Maria taught her family an invaluable lesson: that prioritizing oneself isn't an act of selfishness but of self-love. And in embracing her truth, Maria wasn't just finding herself; she was crafting a legacy of empowerment for all those who shared her life.

In a world brimming with roles and responsibilities, Maria's tale stands out, a beacon of hope. A reminder that amidst the myriad sacrifices, one shouldn't forsake oneself.

Lessons
From Maria's journey, several enlightening lessons can be drawn:

1. **Self-Rediscovery is Vital**: In the hustle of life, it's easy to lose oneself amid responsibilities. However, revisiting and nurturing our passions can lead to profound self-discovery and fulfillment.
2. **Self-Love Isn't Selfishness**: Prioritizing one's own needs and desires doesn't mean neglecting or sidelining those of others. It's essential for mental well-being and personal growth.
3. **Balance, Not Perfection**: A perfect home or a seamless life shouldn't always be the goal. Sometimes, embracing the chaos and finding balance can lead to richer, more fulfilling experiences.
4. **Communication is Key**: Openly sharing feelings and aspirations with loved ones allows them to understand and support our choices. Maria's candidness with her husband about the art class set a precedent.
5. **Lead by Example**: By prioritizing her self-growth, Maria not only benefitted herself but also served as a role model for her children, teaching them about the importance of self-worth and chasing passions.
6. **The Ripple Effect**: Small changes in our personal world, like Maria attending an art class, can lead to broader positive impacts in our shared world, fostering understanding and growth in relationships.
7. **Embrace Evolution**: Life is not static. We evolve, and our roles, desires, and priorities change.

Recognizing and accepting this evolution is vital for personal contentment.

8. **Value of Reflection**: Often, pausing and reflecting on our life's journey can offer invaluable insights. Maria's introspection upon finding her old photograph led her to make life-altering decisions.

These lessons, distilled from Maria's tale, highlight the universality of her experiences and underscore the importance of self-care, understanding, and evolution in our individual lives.

1.3 The Humility of Admission: "Sorry"

"Sorry" — a word so tiny, and yet it possesses a gravitational pull akin to the mightiest of stars. Have you ever paused and wondered how a mere collection of five letters can mend a tear in the fabric of a relationship, or restore a bridge that has been burnt? Its simplicity married with profound depth.

In our fast-paced world, when we stumble, whether it be over a misplaced toy or through a series of misunderstandings with a loved one, our initial reflex is often defense. Our egos, those delicate guardians of our self-worth, immediately raise their shields. Admitting fault? It feels as if you're walking into a cold, unforgiving rain without an umbrella. Vulnerable. Exposed.

Yet, when the rain soaks through, there's an odd sense of catharsis. To say "sorry" is to strip oneself of pretense. It's an acknowledgement, not just of a misdeed or oversight, but of our shared, beautifully imperfect humanity. Sorry isn't a sign of weakness; it's a testament to our strength. Strength to recognize our flaws, to stand in the storm, and to endeavor to be better.

In the realm of relationships, whether familial, romantic, or platonic, the word "sorry" operates much like the reset button on a malfunctioning device. It doesn't erase the error, but it provides an opportunity for a fresh start. It's a salve, an invitation to heal.

Now, imagine a world where the word "sorry" is absent. A world where people move through their days, their mistakes creating ripples that turn into waves, crashing and causing chaos. Sounds tumultuous, right? That's the weight this humble word carries.

You see, "sorry" isn't just about the past or the present—it's a promise for the future. It whispers, "I see my error, and I choose to grow from it."

In conclusion, the magic of "sorry" is wrapped up in its humility and hope. In those moments when it's spoken, time seems to pause, the world softens, and hearts open just a tad wider. It's a word worth cherishing, not for its sorrow, but for the newfound possibilities it births.

James and the Unsent Letter

In a cluttered room with an old wooden desk by the window, James sat with a furrowed brow, an array of memories sprawling out in front of him. He held in his hand a photograph – faded, but the emotions as vivid as yesterday. There he was, a younger James, arm slung around his best friend, Daniel. Their grinning faces captured a shared moment of joy. Yet the memories that weighed him down now were not of their shared laughter, but of the day they had parted in anger.

"I was right," James muttered to himself, staring into the distance. But was he? The deafening weight of pride prevented him from admitting a simple truth. Maybe he wasn't entirely right. Maybe, just maybe, a single word could bridge the yawning chasm between them: "Sorry."

Beneath the photograph, lay an empty page, waiting. It wasn't about admitting defeat or surrendering pride. It was about the humility of recognizing imperfection. With a shaking hand, James began to write, letting the weight of years and unsaid words flow onto the paper.

"Dear Daniel," he scribbled, the words rough and uneven, "I've often replayed that day in my head, our voices raised, our bond strained. While my pride stubbornly shouted 'I was right,' a quiet voice whispered 'But at what cost?'"

He paused, took a deep breath, and wrote, "Sorry."

The letter grew, bursting with memories, regrets, and hopes. It was an admission, not of defeat, but of humanity. It spoke of days gone by and the ache of an empty chair, once occupied by a cherished friend. It spoke of understanding, growth, and the power of a humble heart.

Yet, as the last word was written and the ink dried, James hesitated. The weight of sending it, of laying bare his soul, was overwhelming. And so, the letter remained unsent. But its creation, the very act of writing it, began to mend James's fractured heart.

The letter was a silent testament to the complexity of human emotions. It wasn't about the words but the intent. Even if it never reached Daniel, in James's heart, it was already delivered.

The word "Sorry," so small, yet vast in its implications, is often what stands between healing and hurt. While the world may perceive it as a sign of weakness, in reality, it is an emblem of strength. It takes courage to admit mistakes, humility to understand them, and immense strength to learn from them.

In the dance of life, where pride and ego often lead, "Sorry" is the step that brings us back to the rhythm of love and understanding. It's the echo of a heart willing to mend and be mended. And in that humble admission, in that unsent letter, James found a peace that had eluded him for years.

Lessons
From the tale of "James and the Unsent Letter," several poignant lessons can be learned:

1. **The Weight of Pride**: Pride can be a heavy burden, often preventing us from making amends or even

recognizing our mistakes. It might momentarily protect our ego but at the cost of lasting relationships and inner peace.

2. **Power of Admission**: Admitting a mistake or fault doesn't showcase weakness; rather, it reveals a depth of character, maturity, and understanding. The word "Sorry" is a testament to humility and self-awareness.

3. **The Therapeutic Act of Writing**: Sometimes, just penning down our feelings can be therapeutic. Even if the words never reach their intended recipient, the mere act of expressing can lead to personal healing and clarity.

4. **Introspection and Growth**: It's crucial to sometimes step back and evaluate our actions and the consequences they've borne on our lives. Such introspection often leads to personal growth and a deeper understanding of oneself and others.

5. **Value of Relationships**: Relationships, especially deep-rooted ones, are fragile. It's essential to nurture them and not let misunderstandings or disagreements sever ties permanently.

6. **The Unspoken Impact**: Even unsaid words and actions have a profound effect on our psyche. While James never sent the letter, the mere act of writing it began the healing process, underscoring the impact of internal dialogues and reflections.

7. **Courage in Vulnerability**: Laying one's feelings bare, admitting faults, or reaching out requires

courage. Vulnerability, contrary to popular belief, is a strength, not a weakness.

8. **Regret and Redemption**: Life is too short to live with regrets. While one can't change the past, the present offers a chance for redemption, reconciliation, and rebuilding.

The story of James and his unsent letter underscores the intricate dance of human emotions, the balance between pride and humility, and the ongoing journey of self-awareness and growth.

Chapter 2: Crafting Transparent Communications

Imagine you're in a room filled with smoke. It's thick, suffocating, and you can barely see the person next to you. That, my friend, is the world we live in when we don't communicate transparently. We're enveloped in this smoke of half-truths, vague meanings, and silent expectations. But what if we could clear the air? Let's talk about crafting transparent communications.

You see, words are a bit like LEGO bricks. Simple, colorful, and diverse. Yet, when piled up without design or care, they can become stumbling blocks. Ever stepped on a stray LEGO? Ouch! Similarly, when words are tossed around carelessly, they lead to misunderstandings, missteps, and quite a bit of pain.

But let's rewind. Picture a child with those same LEGO bricks, meticulously crafting a masterpiece. With each piece, a clear image emerges. In communication, that is what we should aim for. Being clear isn't about using big words or crafting perfect sentences. Nope. It's about ensuring the picture in our head matches the one we create in someone else's.

Here's the thing. Have you ever played the game of 'Whisper Down the Lane'? Starts with a simple message, and by the end, it's transformed into something unrecognizable, right? That's the power of non-transparent communication. It's like pouring water into a basket. Pointless and messy.

Transparent communication, on the flip side, is like using a clear glass. You see what's inside. No guesswork, no assumptions. Whether it's talking to your buddy about splitting the dinner bill or telling your colleague about a deadline – being clear saves a ton of headaches.

But wait! Before you think it's all about 'telling it like it is,' there's a secret ingredient: Empathy. Being direct without being kind is like serving plain toast for breakfast. Edible, yes, but hardly satisfying. Season your words with understanding, and suddenly, you have a delightful toast with all the toppings.

To wrap this up (or tie it with a bow, if you fancy that), crafting transparent communications is simple. It's the art of being as clear as a summer's day, with the warmth to match. So, the next time you're about to send that text, make that call, or chat over coffee, remember: Clear the smoke, lay out those LEGO bricks with care, and serve up a delightful toast of words. Because in this vast world of jumbled communications, a little clarity goes a long, long way.

2.1 The Strength in Uncertainty: "I don't know."

In the sleepy town of Elmbridge, the annual trivia night was the highlight of the year. Townsfolk came together, confident in their facts, ready to flaunt their knowledge. Among the eager participants was a young woman named Elsie, often the laughingstock for her frequent admission: "I don't know."

To many, the game was simple: answer the questions, gain points, and wear the crown of the most knowledgeable. But Elsie? She danced to a different rhythm, one that most couldn't quite grasp. With every "I don't know," the crowd would chuckle, but her face beamed with an odd sort of pride.

"Why do you even participate if you don't know?" someone jeered.

Elsie, with a twinkle in her eye, responded, "Because every 'I don't know' is a door waiting to be opened, a mystery waiting to be unraveled."

See, in a world where everyone's racing to have answers, to assert their intellect, Elsie embraced the beauty of uncertainty. There's an unsung power in admitting "I don't know." It doesn't mean one's clueless; it means they're aware that the universe is vast, and our grasp of knowledge, no matter how expansive, is but a speck in the grand scheme.

When Elsie said, "I don't know," she wasn't displaying ignorance but showcasing humility. A humility that whispers, "Teach me, show me, and guide me." There's a burst of potential in every uncertainty, a seed of curiosity that promises growth.

On the outside, it might've seemed like Elsie lost every trivia night, but in reality, she gained something more valuable — the wisdom to admit her limitations, the hunger to learn, and the joy of discovery.

Towards the end of one trivia night, a young boy approached her, eyes wide with admiration. "Miss," he hesitated, "I want to be like you. Not scared of not knowing."

Elsie knelt down, her face level with his, "Then remember, kiddo, 'I don't know' isn't the end but the beginning. It's the first step to a grand adventure."

In Elmbridge, while the trivia night crown passed many heads, Elsie's legacy was the whispered conversations, the raised hands in classrooms, the fearless admissions of "I don't know." She taught the town that strength isn't just in knowing, but in the brave act of admitting when one doesn't, and the journey that follows.

Lena's Unexpected Journey

Lena, a planner by nature, had meticulously marked out every milestone of her life on a physical calendar. One might call it her personal roadmap, and each day was a step closer to her carefully constructed destination. In her life, spontaneity was a mere footnote, a triviality, overshadowed by the bigger picture she'd painted for herself.

But on a crisp autumn morning, the world she knew was turned inside out. With a simple, unopened letter bearing news she hadn't anticipated, her plans unraveled. The job she was sure she'd land, the one she had marked as the next big step? It was no longer an option. The roadmap she'd clung to so tightly was suddenly irrelevant.

The first wave of emotions was a chaotic blend of disbelief and despair. Friends offered their condolences, and family tried to chart out new plans. Everyone seemed to have an answer. Everyone, except Lena. And when asked about her next move, her response was a hesitant, "I don't know."

But in that uncertainty, Lena stumbled upon freedom. No longer shackled by her roadmap, she took a spontaneous trip to a coastal town she'd never heard of. The salty air, the expansive horizon, the rhythmic lull of waves—it was a universe away from her structured life. Lena found herself having impromptu conversations with locals, relishing fresh seafood she'd never tried, and dancing on the beach with nothing but the stars as her audience.

One evening, as she sat by the shoreline, an elderly woman named Mrs. Everly joined her. With her hair the color of the frothy waves and wrinkles mapping out a lifetime of stories, she shared, "You know, dear, some of my best adventures began with 'I don't know.'"

Mrs. Everly's tales were of mistakes turned miracles, unexpected turns leading to unforgettable experiences, and roads less traveled leading to the most treasured destinations. And Lena drank in every word, realizing that "I don't know" wasn't an end but a beginning.

Returning from her trip, Lena's life wasn't magically transformed. But her perspective was. The strength she found in uncertainty became her guiding star. Her roadmap? It remained as a reminder, not of a life planned, but of life lived.

In our quest for certainty, we often forget that life's magic lies in its unpredictability. Lena's journey reminds us that "I don't know" is not an admission of defeat but an embrace of endless possibilities. Sometimes, the most profound growth stems from the seeds of uncertainty. And Lena? She's living proof.

Lessons

From Lena's Unexpected Journey, several lessons emerge that resonate with many facets of the human experience:

1. **Embrace Uncertainty**: Often, we feel the need to have all the answers, believing that certainty equates to stability. However, Lena's story teaches us that there is an inherent strength in embracing the unknown. Uncertainty can pave the way for new experiences and discoveries.

2. **Life is Unpredictable**: No matter how meticulously we plan, life has a way of throwing curveballs. Instead of resisting them, accepting life's unpredictable nature can lead to richer experiences.

3. **Freedom in Letting Go**: By releasing the tight grip on her planned roadmap, Lena found freedom. There's liberation in letting go of rigid expectations and just going with the flow.

4. **Value of Spontaneity**: Sometimes, unplanned adventures can be the most rewarding. They can offer experiences and insights that a structured plan might never have allowed.

5. **Wisdom from Unexpected Sources**: Mrs. Everly, an elderly stranger, offered Lena insights that reshaped her worldview. It's a reminder to remain open to wisdom from unexpected sources; life lessons can come from anyone, anywhere.

6. **Growth Beyond Comfort Zones**: Growth often happens outside of our comfort zones. Facing unfamiliar situations or environments, like Lena's

impromptu coastal trip, can lead to self-discovery and personal development.

7. **"I Don't Know" is Okay**: Admitting "I don't know" is not a sign of weakness but of openness. It signifies a willingness to learn, adapt, and embark on new journeys.

8. **Life Beyond Plans**: While planning is essential, life isn't just about sticking to the script. It's about living in the moment, cherishing the detours, and understanding that sometimes the most beautiful stories are the unplanned ones.

Lena's journey, in essence, speaks to the heart of the human spirit, urging us to embrace the vast spectrum of life with all its uncertainties, surprises, and serendipities.

2.2 Honest Expressions: "I understand you perfectly, and I would like something other."

Honest expressions form the bedrock upon which true understanding and genuine relationships are built. They're more than just forthright words; they're an embodiment of authenticity, vulnerability, and courage. True honesty in communication is the antithesis of pretense, devoid of the facades we often hide behind.

The sentence, "I understand you perfectly, and I would like something other," encapsulates the essence of honest expressions. It gracefully merges two profound notions: comprehension and individual desire.

The first part, "I understand you perfectly," signifies empathy, active listening, and respect. It conveys that one has taken the effort to process and grasp what the other person is communicating. This acknowledgment can be grounding and validating, bridging gaps and fostering connections.

However, the brilliance lies in the continuation: "and I would like something other." This pivot represents a courageous self-awareness and clarity of one's desires. By following up an acknowledgment with a personal preference, it encapsulates the delicate balance of understanding another while honoring one's own feelings and needs.

In various life scenarios, whether choosing a career against traditional familial expectations or navigating personal relationships, such a statement comes in handy. It provides a platform where one doesn't negate the other's perspective but places their own wishes on an equal pedestal.

Imagine being in a restaurant with friends. They all rave about a particular dish and recommend it to you. While you acknowledge their suggestion and appreciate their excitement, you have a different preference for the night. Instead of going with the flow and suppressing your desire, you assert, "I understand you perfectly, and I would like something other."

Such an assertion, while seemingly simple, has profound implications. It encourages open dialogue, ensures mutual respect, and reduces the room for regret or resentment. In relationships, be it familial, platonic, or romantic, such honest expressions can be instrumental in setting boundaries and ensuring mutual respect.

In essence, honest expressions like these emphasize two pillars: deep understanding of the other and a fierce commitment to one's authenticity. By intertwining these two principles, we craft a dialogue that is both compassionate and true, one that allows us to connect deeply while preserving the sanctity of our individuality.

Rob's Dilemma at the Conference

Sunlight streamed in through the towering windows of the grand ballroom, catching the shimmering edge of chandeliers that hung precariously above. The Conference on Global Business Solutions had drawn a veritable who's who from around the world. Rob, in his crisply ironed blue suit, felt a mix of excitement and apprehension. This was his shot to collaborate with the best, to ink deals, and to propel his fledgling startup to new heights.

As presentations unfolded and speakers engaged, the underlying hum of hushed conversations never really ceased. In a corner, sipping on a cup of now lukewarm coffee, Rob found himself in an unexpected, intense conversation with Mrs. Eliza Harrington, the CEO of Harrington Holdings. Her empire had tentacles in almost every industry conceivable, and she was known for her unerring business acumen.

Eliza, with her penetrating blue eyes and silver hair neatly coiled at the nape of her neck, spoke with a clarity and conviction that was hard to dispute. "Rob," she began, her voice soft yet assertive, "Your idea is revolutionary, but I think integrating it with Harrington's existing IT solution will magnify its reach."

Rob listened, each word a feather adding weight to the scale of decision. The proposal, while lucrative, was a far cry from his vision. He took a deep breath, the ambient sounds of the conference melting into a distant murmur. How easy it would be to nod, to agree, and to let the tidal wave of Eliza's influence carry him forward.

But then, the very essence of his startup flashed before him — nights spent brainstorming, the first code he wrote, the dreams, and the passion. The gut-wrenching reality of this decision became painfully clear. This was not just about business; it was about staying true to himself and his vision.

"I understand you perfectly," he began, locking eyes with Eliza, "and I have immense respect for Harrington Holdings. But, I would like something other. My vision for my startup is distinct, and I feel this integration might dilute that."

Silence hung thick, punctuated only by the distant echo of applause from the stage. Rob's heart raced, unsure if he had just made the biggest mistake of his life or taken the bravest stand of his career.

Eliza stared at him for what felt like an eternity before her lips curled into a slight smile. "It's not often," she said slowly, "that someone speaks their mind so honestly to me. Let's see how we can maintain the essence of your vision and still collaborate. Because Rob, that's a fire in you, and I'd hate to see it extinguished."

As the day wrapped, amidst the handshakes and exchanged business cards, Rob's simple act of honest expression stood out, shimmering brighter than the chandeliers above. For in a world driven by profit and power, he was reminded of the unmatched value of authenticity.

Chapter 3: Liberation through Emotional Honesty

In the heart of a bustling city, amid the daily symphony of honking cars, hasty footsteps, and muted conversations, there's an alley. Not particularly remarkable, overshadowed by towering buildings, its bricks aged by time and neglect. But on a peculiar evening, the sun's golden hue dappled through the leaves, turning this ordinary alley into a corridor of revelations.

Ever noticed how the sun doesn't pretend to shine? It just does. There's an uncanny similarity between the sun and our emotions. Emotions, raw and untamed, are much like those sunbeams – they seek an outlet, a crack, a tiny space to seep through and manifest. But often, in the hustle and dance of life, we build walls, tall and impenetrable, not just around us, but within us. Behind these walls, we stash away our true feelings, suppressing the whispers of our heart, muffling our inner cries.

However, have you ever felt the sheer weight of a held-back tear or the tight clasp of an unsaid word? It's like holding a balloon underwater. The pressure, the tension – it's palpable. But what if, just for a moment, we allowed that balloon to surface? What if we allowed ourselves the raw, unbridled luxury of emotional honesty?

Sarah did. Sarah, a 28-year-old accountant, lived life by the book. Timelines, charts, predictability - these were her sanctuaries. Until one evening, in that sun-kissed alley, a stray cat approached her, its eyes brimming with a melancholy she recognized all too well. Without a second thought, she knelt and held the feline, letting tears she hadn't known were there, stream down. It wasn't about the cat. It was about every stifled emotion, every 'I'm fine' when she wasn't, every smile masking a storm.

There's an unparalleled freedom in being emotionally honest. It's like taking a deep breath after being underwater for too long. It's the gusty laughter after a good cry, the warmth of an embrace, the release of a long-held sigh. The world might tell us to hold it together, to be strong, to conceal. But strength isn't just in holding on; sometimes, it's in letting go.

Imagine a world where we could be our most genuine selves, where 'How are you?' isn't just a greeting, but a heartfelt inquiry, and 'I'm not okay' is as accepted as 'I'm fine'. It's not just about liberation; it's about connection, authenticity, and the profound joy of being seen, heard, and understood.

Because, in the end, liberation through emotional honesty isn't just about breaking chains; it's about weaving bonds - bonds with oneself and with the world.

And as the sun set on that alley, Sarah walked out, a little lighter, a little freer, and infinitely more herself.

3.1 Self-Forgiveness: "I better forgive myself for that right away."

Mistakes. We all make them. In the grand tapestry of life, they're the knots, the jumbled threads, the unexpected colors that sometimes seem out of place. Think of young Tommy, who once "borrowed" a candy bar from the corner store. Or Susan, who promised to attend her best friend's recital but forgot. Big or small, we've all been there.

Ever noticed how when others stumble, we rush in with, "It's okay. It happens." But when it's our own misstep, our inner critic unleashes a storm? Why did I do that? How could I be so careless? The echoes of these reprimands bounce around, growing louder and more persistent.

Enter the magic words: "I better forgive myself for that right away." They're not a get-out-of-jail-free card, nor an excuse to avoid responsibility. Instead, they're an acknowledgment. They say, "Yes, I messed up, but I am more than this single error. I won't let it define me."

Imagine holding onto every stone of regret you've ever stumbled upon. With time, these stones transform into boulders. They weigh us down, make our steps hesitant, our paths meandering. But self-forgiveness? It's the act of setting down those boulders, giving our souls the space to breathe, to heal.

Let's be real. No one's perfect. Not even close. Those Instagram models? They've got their insecurities. That neighbor with the perfect lawn? He's battling his own demons. Forgiving oneself isn't about ignoring flaws but recognizing that growth comes from acceptance. From understanding. From love.

It's like rain after a particularly parched summer. First, a drizzle, hesitant and gentle. Then, the downpour, cleansing and rejuvenating. That's self-forgiveness. It's the rain that washes away the accumulated dust of self-doubt, allowing the green shoots of self-worth to break through.

So, the next time you're in the midst of a mental face palm, take a deep breath. And remember: "I better forgive myself for that right away." For it's in those moments of grace towards ourselves, that we find the strength to move forward, lighter and with purpose. Remember, every sunrise promises a new start. Your heart deserves its own dawn too.

Sarah's Forgotten Birthday

Sunlight streamed into Sarah's bedroom, casting a golden halo around everything it touched. The playful chirping of birds outside was nature's serenade for a special day—Sarah's birthday. She rose from her bed with a stretch and a hopeful smile, eagerly waiting for the influx of birthday messages and calls.

By noon, the anticipation started to weigh her down. She had always been the planner, the rememberer, the one who made birthdays special for everyone around her. From throwing surprise parties to finding the perfect gifts, Sarah was the heart behind countless birthday memories. This year, she had deliberately left the planning to others, wanting to experience that same joy. And yet, the day passed quietly, with no buzzes or notifications.

As the sun dipped below the horizon, sadness morphed into self-blame. Thoughts began to swirl in her mind. "Maybe I expect too much," she thought, tears brimming. "Perhaps my worth is tied to how much I give and not who I am."

But then, amid the spiraling thoughts, a flicker of clarity emerged. She recalled the sentence she'd read in a self-help book, "I better forgive myself for that right away." It wasn't her fault that people forgot. It wasn't even entirely their fault. People are so engrossed in the hustle and bustle of life that they often miss the small things—even if those small things are as big as a dear friend's birthday.

That night, Sarah sat down with a piece of cake, lit a candle, and sang to herself. She made a wish, not for gifts or surprise parties, but for self-love and forgiveness. The kind of forgiveness that mends the spirit and renews the soul.

Because at the end of the day, while it's nice to be celebrated by others, it's essential to celebrate oneself. And part of that celebration is forgiving yourself for mistakes, for high expectations, and for every little thing that may not go as planned.

Months later, when recounting the story to a friend, she'd say, "You know, that birthday was a gift. Not wrapped in ribbons or concealed in a box, but in understanding, growth, and self-love."

The narrative of Sarah's forgotten birthday isn't just about a day that went unnoticed. It's a testament to the art of self-forgiveness, of understanding our worth beyond external validations, and finding peace in the symphony of our own heartbeats. After all, the first step to feeling loved by the world is to embrace and forgive oneself, completely and unconditionally.

Lessons

1. **Self-worth Isn't Defined by External Validation**: Often, we tether our self-worth to how others perceive or celebrate us. Sarah's journey serves as

a reminder that our worth isn't contingent upon external recognitions but is intrinsic and unwavering.

2. **Forgiveness Begins Within**: Before we seek forgiveness or understanding from others, we must offer it to ourselves. This act isn't just about absolving our perceived faults but also about embracing our humaneness.

3. **Expectations Can Lead to Disappointment**: While it's natural to have expectations, especially from those close to us, it's essential to recognize that they can sometimes lead to unintended disappointments. The key lies in balancing hopes with a sense of reality and understanding.

4. **Celebrate Yourself**: In a world where we often wait for others to recognize or celebrate us, it's crucial to understand the importance of self-celebration. Treating ourselves, acknowledging our achievements, or even just taking a moment to appreciate our journey is invaluable.

5. **Life's Unplanned Moments Can Offer the Most Profound Insights**: It wasn't the birthday Sarah had imagined, but it gave her a perspective and growth that might not have emerged from a typical birthday celebration. Sometimes, it's the unplanned, unexpected moments that offer the deepest insights and memories.

6. **The Importance of Self-Love**: Loving oneself is the foundation for genuine happiness and fulfillment. When things don't go as planned, or when we face

moments of doubt, it's this self-love that acts as a beacon, guiding us back to inner peace.

7. **People Aren't Flawless**: Humans, by nature, are forgetful, engrossed in their challenges, or simply unaware. It's essential to remember this when feelings of neglect or disappointment arise. Understanding this can make the journey of forgiveness easier.

In essence, Sarah's story underscores the imperfections of life and relationships but also highlights the transformative power of introspection, self-love, and forgiveness.

3.2 Staying True to Feelings: "I'm just realizing that the subject doesn't really interest me."

In the kaleidoscope of life, amidst the myriad colors and patterns, there lies an uncharted territory, often subdued and silenced – our true feelings.

Imagine, for a moment, being seated in a cozy, dim-lit room. There's a gentle hum of conversation, punctuated by the clinking of glasses. You're amidst people, some familiar, some not so much, and they're all engrossed in a passionate discussion about, let's say, the delicate nuances of 18th-century European art. The fervor is palpable. The air, thick with enthusiasm. And there you are, nodding in polite agreement, your mind, however, adrift. Maybe you're thinking about the moon, or the spicy tang of the taco you had last night, or that song that's been stuck in your head. And then, like a bubble bursting, comes the realization: "I'm just realizing that the subject doesn't really interest me."

There's an inherent beauty in this confession. It's not a statement of ignorance or indifference. It's an acknowledgment, a gentle acceptance of one's own emotional landscape. In a world that often pushes us to conform, to fit into neatly labeled boxes, the courage to admit our true feelings, especially when they go against the grain, is a revolutionary act. It's like finally exhaling after holding your breath for far too long.

Yet, there's often a cloud of hesitation that overshadows such admissions. "What would they think?" "Would this make me seem ignorant?" "Am I the odd one out?" But here's the twist: Life isn't a scripted play. It's a spontaneous, ever-evolving dance, and there's no choreography that can match the authenticity of your own rhythm.

Remember that summer afternoon when you were a child? The world beckoned you with open arms. The sky, a canvas of azure and gold. There was no room for pretense, no thought of what's "right" or "popular." You just followed your heart, maybe chasing after butterflies or laying on the grass, lost in a world of dreams. That child, unabashed and unfiltered, is still a part of you. And every time you stay true to your feelings, you let that child take the lead, reminding you of the simplicity and honesty that life was, and can still be.

"I'm just realizing that the subject doesn't really interest me." It's not just a sentence; it's a doorway. A doorway to vulnerability, to authenticity, and, most importantly, to yourself. So, the next time you're amidst the hum and clink, lost in thoughts of tacos, moons, or melodies, take a moment. Breathe. And let your heart speak its truth, in all its perplexing, bursting glory.

Mike's Unwanted Art Class

Mike's life was a canvas of predictable hues — a steady job, a comfortable routine, and an occasional game night with friends. However, on his 30th birthday, a gift from his well-meaning sister threatened to introduce an unexpected splash of color: art classes.

The room was a bright riot of colors, with light filtering through stained glass windows, casting kaleidoscopic patterns on the hardwood floor. Aromas of oil paint and fresh canvas filled the air, and hushed conversations surrounded him. Students, many of them a decade or so younger, chatted animatedly about the world of art.

Mike sat stiffly on a stool, facing a blank canvas that seemed to mock his lack of experience. With every stroke he made, his discomfort grew. Around him, students painted with ease, their brushes dancing across the canvas, bringing to life scenes of rolling hills, bustling streets, and serene waters. Mike's canvas, on the other hand, was a mix of smudged lines and unclear shapes.

The teacher, Mrs. Gallagher, a petite woman with silver hair and a spark in her eyes, approached him. "Mike, loosen up! Let the brush flow. Let it tell your story."

He tried. He truly did. He recalled landscapes from his childhood, tried to paint memories, but it all felt... forced.

With every passing class, the weight of the canvas seemed heavier, and the colors more distant.

One evening, after an especially frustrating session, Mrs. Gallagher sat beside him. "What's on your mind, Mike?"

Taking a deep breath, he replied, "I'm just realizing that the subject doesn't really interest me."

Mrs. Gallagher looked at him, her eyes reflecting understanding. "Art," she began slowly, "isn't always about painting or creating masterpieces. It's about expressing oneself, finding a passion. Maybe this isn't your medium, and that's okay."

Mike nodded. "I thought I'd grow to love it, especially seeing everyone else so involved. But it feels like I'm pretending, wearing a mask."

She smiled gently. "Life's too short for that, Mike. Take this as a lesson to stay true to yourself. Find your canvas, wherever it may be, and paint your story there."

Mike left the class, not with a masterpiece in his hand, but with a lesson etched in his heart. He realized that sometimes, it's not about fitting into someone else's world but about creating one's own. Not every canvas needs paint; sometimes, it's the brush, the strokes, and the heartfelt emotions that matter.

Life is filled with myriad experiences, each teaching us something invaluable. Mike's story is a testament to that. Amidst societal expectations and the cacophony of choices, it's essential to pause, reflect, and stay true to our feelings, even if it means admitting that something isn't quite right for us.

Lessons

1. **Self-awareness is paramount:** Instead of persistently trying to fit into a mold that isn't meant for him, Mike's realization that the art class wasn't his passion underscores the importance of understanding oneself and one's genuine interests.

2. **Not every experience has to be embraced:** While it's beneficial to try new things, it's equally vital to recognize when something doesn't resonate with us. Every individual has their unique canvas in life, and not every medium or subject will be the right fit.

3. **It's okay to say "no":** Mike's candid confession to Mrs. Gallagher demonstrates that admitting our true feelings, even if they don't align with what's expected, is a strength and not a weakness.

4. **Life's true essence is authenticity:** Mike's journey from trying to enjoy the class to understanding his real feelings emphasizes the need for authenticity in our pursuits. Life is too short to spend on things that don't ignite passion or joy within us.

5. **Growth comes from unexpected places:** While the art class may not have turned Mike into an artist, it became a medium for him to learn a crucial life lesson about staying true to oneself.

In essence, Mike's journey in the unwanted art class serves as a reminder that, in the grand tapestry of life, it's vital to choose threads that resonate with our true self, weaving a story that is both genuine and fulfilling

Chapter 4: Valuing Personal Space

Imagine, if you will, a garden. In the heart of it, stands a tree—tall, robust, and flourishing. But for this tree to thrive, it doesn't just need sunlight, water, or nourishing soil. It requires space. Space to spread its roots, stretch its branches, and dance freely to the whispers of the wind.

Personal space, much like that space in our imaginary garden, is not just the distance we enjoy from others physically. It's a refuge, a little nook in the universe where our thoughts can swirl, and emotions can ebb and flow without interference. We need it. Just like our tree, we too, need room to grow, ponder, and simply be.

Yet, in today's bustling world of never-ending notifications, overcrowded subways, and the societal pressure of eternal availability, this space often shrinks, sometimes to the point of non-existence. We are swiped, pinged, and beeped into a constant state of alertness, often at the cost of our inner peace.

But here's the catch. Personal space isn't a luxury—it's a necessity. It's as vital as air. Just as a bird needs the vast sky to spread its wings, our souls, our minds, need that metaphorical room to breathe, to reflect, and occasionally, to retreat. It's in these quiet moments of solitude that we often find our most profound insights, our deepest emotions, and our purest form of self.

But how does one carve out this space in a world that is always encroaching?

Sometimes, it's about drawing a boundary—a polite, yet firm stance on when to answer that call, or when to indulge in the luxury of disconnecting. Other times, it's about taking a deliberate pause—a walk in the park, a silent evening with a book, or even a momentary gaze out of the window. And, quite often, it's about communication, letting those around you understand and respect your need for that little cocoon of calm.

In essence, valuing personal space is a dance—a dance of balance between engagement and solitude, between sharing and introspecting. It's not about isolation but rejuvenation.

4.1 The Need for Solitude: "I'd rather be on my own right now."

Solitude - often mistaken for loneliness, is a balm. But it's so much more than just an antidote to the noise. It's a refuge, where the mind finds space to untangle the knots of thoughts. Think of a potter at the wheel. As the clay spins and molds, it requires pauses. Those pauses aren't empty – they're full of intention, observation, and recalibration.

The need for solitude is not an affront to company; it's an embrace of oneself. It's in those silent moments, devoid of external judgments and disturbances, that one reconnects with their core, remembers forgotten dreams, and relishes the simplicity of being. To say, "I'd rather be on my own right now," is to honor the relationship one has with oneself, to treasure the sanctity of silent introspection.

Just as the earth needs the gentle caress of the night to rejuvenate, so does the human spirit, every once in a while, long for the solace of solitude.

Emily's Weekend Retreat

The hush of the wind, whispering tales of long-forgotten times, the rustle of the autumn leaves, mimicking a soft serenade, and in the midst of this orchestral beauty stood Emily, with the weight of the world on her fragile shoulders. The city's relentless cacophony, its insistent demands, and the ceaseless dance of responsibilities had begun to take a toll on her. Emily's heart ached for a reprieve, a momentary escape where her thoughts weren't drowned out by the mechanical humdrum of modern life.

There's a peculiar intensity in the eyes of someone who craves solitude. It's a silent scream, an unvoiced plea, a deep-seated yearning to momentarily disconnect, to introspect. And it was this intensity that was burning bright in Emily's hazel eyes as she stood on the porch of a quaint wooden cabin nestled deep within the heart of the Smoky Mountains.

The world saw Emily as a vibrant social butterfly. She was the life of every party, the confidante to many, and the go-to person for advice, laughter, and solace. Yet, very few understood the depth of her introspective nature, her need to recharge, to retreat within herself, and rediscover her core.

As Emily walked into the forest, each step took her further from the world's clutches and closer to her soul. The birds' melodious songs resonated with her thoughts, and the gentle brook mirrored her fluid emotions. With every tree she passed, she shed a layer of societal expectation, a preconceived notion, a label.

There, amid nature's embrace, her epiphany came with the soft glow of twilight. The world, for all its beauty and chaos, often blurred the lines of individuality. Solitude wasn't a mere luxury; it was essential. A necessity to maintain the equilibrium of one's soul. In the absence of external voices, she could finally hear her own, whispering secrets, dreams, and desires she'd long forgotten.

By Sunday evening, the cabin had witnessed a metamorphosis. Emily emerged not as a transformed individual, but as someone who had peeled away the layers of noise, expectations, and pretense to reveal her authentic self. She was rejuvenated, centered, and had a shimmering clarity of purpose.

To the world, it might have been just a weekend retreat, but for Emily, it was a journey of reconnection, introspection, and profound self-discovery. And as she drove back to the bustling city, her heart carried a simple, yet powerful sentence, a beacon for future introspections: "I'd rather be on my own right now." Because in solitude, Emily had found her most evocative symphony.

Lessons

1. **The Power of Solitude:** In today's hyper-connected world, solitude is not a sign of loneliness but a choice for self-reflection and rejuvenation. Taking time alone allows us to disconnect from external

distractions and connect deeply with our inner selves.

2. **Beyond External Perceptions:** No matter how the world perceives an individual, only they truly understand their needs and desires. While Emily was seen as an outgoing social butterfly, she also had a deep-seated need for introspection.

3. **Nature as a Healing Force:** The natural world, with its serene landscapes and harmonious sounds, can be a powerful force for mental and emotional healing. It offers an environment devoid of man-made distractions, allowing for profound self-discovery.

4. **Self-Rediscovery:** Over time, the weight of societal expectations and roles can cloud our true selves. It's essential to periodically shed these layers and reacquaint ourselves with who we genuinely are and what we truly desire.

5. **Balance in Life:** Just as we need social interactions and engagements, we also need moments of solitude. Achieving a balance between the two is crucial for holistic well-being.

6. **Listening to Inner Voices:** Often, the hustle and bustle of life drown out our inner voices. By prioritizing solitude, we give ourselves a chance to truly listen to our thoughts, dreams, and desires.

7. **The Strength in Vulnerability:** Embracing solitude and confronting one's feelings and thoughts requires courage. It's in these vulnerable moments that true strength and clarity emerge.

8. **The Value of Moments:** Every moment, whether spent in solitude or with others, has intrinsic value. It's essential to recognize and cherish these moments, as they shape our understanding and experience of life.

In essence, Emily's story underscores the importance of self-awareness, the healing power of nature, and the transformative potential of solitude. It serves as a gentle reminder that amidst our busy lives, pausing to introspect and reconnect with ourselves can be a profound and enriching experience.

4.2 Accountability: "Pointing fingers is pointing three fingers at oneself."

A balmy afternoon in mid-July, the park buzzed with children's laughter, families picnicking, and birds chirping in an almost orchestrated cacophony. Amidst this idyllic setting, young Liam stood, teary-eyed and ruffled, pointing an accusatory finger at his friend, Jenny. His ice cream lay splattered on the ground, a chocolate puddle melting away, much like his hopes of a sweet treat.

But take a closer look at Liam's hand. As one finger stretched towards Jenny, three fingers curled back towards himself. This physical reality reflects a deeper, poignant truth about the nature of blame and responsibility.

Blaming is, for many, an instinctual defensive reaction, almost a protective shield against the vulnerabilities of being wrong or facing the repercussions of our actions. We are, by design, more apt to see the mote in another's eye and overlook the beam in our own. Yet, when we hastily cast blame, we often ignore a trinity of truths pointing back at us: our role in the situation, the opportunity to introspect, and the chance to grow from the experience.

Imagine if Liam paused, even for a fleeting moment, to consider: Did he recklessly run around, making it easier for his ice cream to be knocked over? Could this be an opportunity to understand that accidents happen, even amidst the joys of summer days and friendly tussles? Or, perhaps, this was a chance for him to learn the grace of forgiveness, both towards Jenny and towards himself.

Our lives are peppered with "Liam moments". Moments where blame seems easier than reflection, where pointing fingers feels more comforting than baring our hearts and accepting our part. Yet, in the shadow of blame lies the vast horizon of accountability, urging us to look beyond the immediacy of hurt and embrace the expansive growth of understanding.

In the intricate dance of life, accountability is the rhythm that keeps us grounded, a silent reminder that while it's easy to point outwards, true wisdom lies in the journey inwards. It's not just about an ice cream or a fleeting disappointment. It's about recognizing that every time we extend our finger to accuse, three fingers invite us to introspect, to grow, and to be better.

For in the grand theater of life, true victory isn't in pinpointing where others went wrong, but in understanding where we can set things right.

The Office Blame Game

The golden morning sun cast its illuminating rays through the large windows of the Sycamore Corp, giving life to the sterile white walls. It was the kind of workplace that reverberated with the tap-tap of keyboards, where the aroma of fresh coffee mingled with the undertones of ambition. But that particular morning, something was amiss. Whispers snaked around cubicles and conversations huddled in corners. A crucial project had failed, and the hunt for the responsible party was in full swing.

Jeremy, the team lead, was a tall man with a penchant for crisp white shirts and ties that always seemed a shade too bright. His usually composed face was now knitted with worry. He had been in back-to-back meetings, and his normally jovial eyes hid a storm. Conversations were no longer about finding a solution but were veering dangerously close to the treacherous territory of the blame game.

"I had sent those reports to Susan last week!" Mark's voice rose defensively.

"And I clearly asked Rachel for the numbers," Susan retorted, her face flushed.

Rachel, a newbie, could only stammer, "I thought Tim was on it."

Amid the cacophony of accusations, an old voice pierced through. It was Mr. Whittaker, the oldest employee of Sycamore Corp, known more for his silence than his speech. The room fell eerily silent, every gaze fixed on him.

He cleared his throat, his voice steady but laden with wisdom. "When you point a finger at someone, three fingers point back at you." The room was still. "We are not just colleagues. We are cogs in the vast machinery of this corporation. When one fails, we all falter. Instead of finding whom to blame, let's discover where we went wrong."

Mr. Whittaker's words were like a cold splash of water on a summer day — shocking yet refreshing. The tempest of emotions that had gripped the room started to wane. Jeremy, looking both humbled and enlightened, took a deep breath. "Alright, team. Let's regroup, understand our gaps, and rectify them. Together."

Weeks later, as the office corridors buzzed with the successful completion of the project, there was a newfound respect in the air. Not just for Mr. Whittaker and his profound words, but for the beauty of collective accountability.

The incident served as a poignant reminder: it's easy to blame, but true growth emerges from introspection. For in the maze of pointing fingers, the path to progress is often lost. But when one understands that three fingers always point back, the journey becomes less about blame and more about collective growth. Because accountability, much like success, is a team sport.

Chapter 5: Insights into Decisions and Judgments

Imagine, for a moment, standing at the edge of a vast, echoing canyon. Below you, the paths crisscross and intertwine like the veins on a leaf, each one representing a decision, a choice, a judgment. As you stand there, the breeze carries whispers of past choices, echoing with the 'could-haves' and 'should-haves'. But, here's the thing about decisions: they're as fleeting as that very breeze and as powerful as the canyon's formidable depths.

Every choice we make, every judgment we cast, carves a unique imprint on the tapestry of our lives. But what drives us to choose one path over another? Sometimes its logic, sometimes its gut feeling, and at times, it's the haunting memories of past choices, urging us to tread differently.

In the dappled sunlight of morning, Clara, a young woman of vibrant spirit, once told me about her most perplexing decision. "It was like choosing between a comforting, warm blanket and a thrilling, unpredictable adventure," she whispered with a tinge of nostalgia. Her eyes, brimming with wisdom, bore into mine, and she said, "Decisions, in their essence, are the silent narrators of our stories."

But here's the rub: judgments are the specters that often linger in the backdrop. They're the unsolicited guests at our dinner table, silently watching, analyzing. Whether it's the judgment we cast upon others, the world, or the harsher ones we reserve for ourselves, they shape our perceptions, our interactions, and our very being.

For who hasn't felt the sting of regret over a hastily made decision? Or the burn of a judgment too quickly passed? Yet, paradoxically, it's in these very moments that we find our most profound insights. Like the sudden burst of color in a monochrome painting or the unexpected high note in a melancholic symphony.

Life's tapestry is woven with threads of decisions and embroidered with patterns of judgments. But here's the marvel - every stitch, every twist, and every turn holds the promise of insight, of understanding. And if we're willing to stop, listen, and reflect, we might just discern the soft heartbeat of wisdom echoing in the canyon of our choices.

So, as you tread life's intricate pathways, remember: decisions give direction, judgments offer perspective, and insights? They're the soulful melodies that make the journey unforgettable.

5.1 Choosing Activeness: "I can't afford not to do this."

In the sprawling canvas of life, filled with myriad colors and shades, one phrase stands out stark and clear: "I can't afford not to do this." It's not just about money or resources. It's about time, emotion, and the essence of life itself.

Imagine for a moment, a tightrope walker suspended high above a cityscape. Every step she takes requires precision, balance, and immense courage. One misstep and the consequences could be dire. But why does she choose this perilous path? Because for her, the thrill of the challenge, the feeling of flying, and the triumph of reaching the other side outweigh the potential pitfalls. In her heart, she believes, "I can't afford not to do this." She chooses activeness over passive acceptance.

Activeness is the conscious choice to engage with life. It's about taking the reins in our hands, making decisions that push boundaries and challenge the status quo. It's about not letting fear dictate our path, but instead allowing passion, conviction, and purpose to guide our way.

Consider Mark, a young man from a small town with dreams larger than the sprawling fields that surrounded him. He yearned to venture out, to study in a city university, even when everyone cautioned against it. "It's too risky," they said. "You won't fit in," warned others.

But Mark had a fire within. He knew, deep down, that if he didn't pursue this dream, he'd always wonder "what if?" For him, the cost of not taking action was far greater than any potential risks. He believed, "I can't afford not to do this."

Choosing activeness isn't about being reckless or impulsive. It's about acknowledging that every decision, or lack thereof, comes with a cost. Sometimes, the cost of inaction, of letting opportunities slip by, of not pursuing our passions, is far greater than any risks we might face.

In a world where it's easy to be swept away by the currents of doubt, inertia, and apprehension, choosing activeness is an affirmation of one's belief in oneself. It's a commitment to one's dreams, aspirations, and potentials. When we say, "I can't afford not to do this," we're not just making a statement; we're making a choice - a choice to live actively, passionately, and unapologetically.

Sam's Start-up Challenge

Sam had always been what most would consider a 'by-the-book' guy. Steady job at a reputable firm, decent paycheck, and the predictable rhythm of 9 to 5. However, deep inside, the embers of an idea were slowly burning— a startup idea that he believed could revolutionize the world of e-commerce.

As days turned into months, the idea's pull grew stronger. It whispered in his ears during board meetings, it nudged him at the dinner table, and it screamed at him in the quiet of the night. There were challenges, of course: the daunting world of entrepreneurship, the risks of leaving a stable job, the skepticism from peers, and the looming possibility of failure.

One day, after an especially grueling workday, Sam found himself staring at the many business plans and notes he had jotted down for his start-up. And in that moment of introspection, the magnitude of what he was contemplating weighed down on him. But amid the cacophony of doubts and fears, a simple clarity emerged, a sentence that would guide his journey henceforth: "I can't afford not to do this."

It wasn't just about financial implications or societal expectations. It was about his own sense of self, his passion, and the possibility of regret. The activeness of pursuing a dream, despite the mountains of challenges, felt more essential than the passive safety of his current life.

Choosing activeness for Sam was not about dismissing caution but rather recognizing the greater risk in not chasing one's dreams. It was about understanding that life's true value wasn't in the accolades and comforts but in the journeys undertaken, in the risks braved, and in the stories crafted.

In the months that followed, Sam faced his fair share of challenges, from funding issues to operational hiccups. But every time an obstacle reared its head, Sam's mantra reverberated in his mind, fueling his resolve.

And while the world saw the birth of yet another startup, for Sam, it was the birth of a new self—a version that chose activity over passivity, dreams over doubts, and the unknown over the known

5.2 Shifting Perspectives: "I think that says more about you than about me."

Life is like standing before a grand, intricately designed mirror. Every experience, emotion, and interaction we encounter reflects back to us in varying shades and interpretations. But, here's the catch: the image isn't just of us, but also a culmination of the beholder's perceptions, biases, and histories.

Consider an instance where someone says, "You're always so quiet. It must be so boring inside your head." Now, this comment, intended or unintended, carries a hint of judgment. The immediate reaction might be to defend oneself or feel insulted. However, the phrase "I think that says more about you than about me" gifts us a moment of clarity and self-assurance.

This statement isn't about being combative; it's about understanding the depth of perspectives. It signifies that often, when people pass judgments or make assumptions, they are projecting their own insecurities, beliefs, or experiences onto others. What they see or choose to comment on is, more often than not, a reflection of their inner world rather than an accurate representation of the person they are commenting on.

Let's delve a bit deeper. When someone labels you as 'too quiet,' perhaps they're uncomfortable with silence, equating it with awkwardness or emptiness. Their discomfort says more about their own relationship with silence than it does about your character or thought process.

By shifting our perspective and recognizing this, we can navigate life with greater empathy and self-assuredness. We learn not to internalize every critique or opinion thrown our way. We start to see comments, especially unsolicited ones, as windows into the souls of others rather than critiques of our own.

So, the next time you find yourself at the receiving end of a hasty judgment, remember, life's mirror has two faces. And sometimes, it's not you being reflected, but the person standing right beside you.

Clara's Debate with her Father

It was a Sunday evening, the kind where the orange sunbeams tried to peek through the half-drawn curtains of the living room. Clara, a spirited twenty-something, and her father, Mr. Mitchell, sat across each other. The coffee table between them bore two mugs of steaming coffee, and an air of tension you could almost touch.

Mr. Mitchell had always been the traditional kind, holding onto beliefs passed down through generations. Clara, on the other hand, was the embodiment of modernity. She questioned conventions, celebrated diversity, and believed in carving out her own path. Their conversations often seemed like two distinct melodies trying to find a common beat.

On this particular day, they were debating about Clara's decision to take a gap year and travel. Mr. Mitchell found the idea reckless. "Back in my day, we'd finish school, find a job, and stick to it," he began, his voice carrying the weight of his convictions. "This wandering around, seeking 'oneself', it's all a distraction from responsibility."

Clara, taking a deep breath and choosing her words carefully, responded, "Dad, I understand where you're coming from. But times have changed. Experiences shape us, and there's a world out there I want to see, cultures I want to immerse in. I don't want to look back and regret not giving myself this chance."

Her father, a hint of exasperation in his voice, retorted, "You always want to swim against the tide, Clara. Why can't you just do things the simple, tried and tested way?"

And that's when Clara, calm yet assertive, said the line that would change the course of their conversation, "I think that says more about you than about me."

There was a momentary silence. Those words weren't an attack but a mirror. Clara was highlighting the fact that often our responses and judgments are a reflection of our own fears, biases, and experiences, rather than an objective assessment of another's choice.

Mr. Mitchell looked deep into his coffee, perhaps seeing past memories and his own youthful dreams in its dark depths. The room was silent, save for the ticking clock and distant city sounds.

Finally, he spoke, softer now, "Maybe you're right. Maybe I've been looking at things only from my viewpoint. I just worry about you."

Clara leaned in, taking her father's hand, "I know you do. And I cherish that. But sometimes, shifting our perspective, understanding that we all have different journeys, can make these conversations easier."

The evening turned into night, and while Clara and Mr. Mitchell didn't magically see eye-to-eye on everything, they both recognized the power of perspective. Sometimes, understanding isn't about agreeing, but about seeing beyond one's own reflections and truly listening to the other.

Chapter 6: Diplomacy in Disagreements

Imagine, for a moment, two ships in a fierce storm. The waves are tumultuous, the wind howling. Each captain has their own course set, convinced their direction is right. They shout across the waters, the thunder drowning their voices. Neither can hear the other. The storm rages on, and so do they.

Now, picture this: instead of shouting, one captain raises a white flag and signals to meet midway, to talk. This simple act doesn't mean surrender, but a pause—a brief, silent moment to communicate and understand. This is diplomacy in disagreements.

Life's disagreements can be those roaring storms. We're all captains of our own ships, navigating through the vast sea of opinions, beliefs, and emotions. There's Aunt Mabel, with her staunch political views over Thanksgiving dinner; or Bob from the office, who believes coffee should always be black. Differences are inevitable. But how we address these differences can change the course of our journeys.

Diplomacy isn't about diluting your beliefs. It's about recognizing that another's viewpoint doesn't diminish your own. It's the delicate dance of words where listening becomes as essential as speaking. Here, tone softens, the pace slows, and respect replaces retaliation. It's the art of seeking understanding over victory.

But why bother? Why not ride the storm and let the chips fall where they may?

Because relationships are treasures. They're fragile, intricate webs spun over time, experiences, and shared memories. Diplomacy in disagreements acts as the balm that prevents the wear and tear, the frays and the breaks. It's the unsung hero in tales of lifelong friendships, harmonious families, and successful boardroom meetings.

Remember the two ships? They could easily clash, letting the storm dictate their fate. Or, they can find calm waters, converse, and maybe discover that while their destinations are different, the stars guiding them share the same sky.

So, the next time a storm brews, ask yourself: Do I let the winds sway me? Or do I choose to steer with grace, understanding, and diplomacy? Because sometimes, the mightiest thing isn't to stand against the storm, but to find a way to sail together through it.

6.1. The Peace Pact: "Let's agree that we don't agree."

"The Peace Pact: 'Let's agree that we don't agree'" is a phrase that embodies the principle of mutual respect amidst differences. Let's break it down for better understanding:

The Peace Pact: A pact is typically an agreement or a treaty between two or more parties. By referring to this agreement as a "peace" pact, it emphasizes that the intent is harmony and understanding rather than continued conflict.

"Let's agree": This part of the phrase denotes mutual consensus. It suggests that both parties are on the same page about the following statement, indicating a shared understanding or decision.

"That we don't agree": This is an acknowledgment of differences in opinion, belief, or perspective. It means both parties recognize that they have conflicting views on a subject.

When combined, the whole sentence communicates a profound idea: It's possible to have differences with someone but still maintain respect and understanding. Instead of continuing a potentially endless argument where neither party changes their viewpoint, this phrase offers a solution—to consciously accept the difference in opinions and move forward.

In essence, "Let's agree that we don't agree" is a call for tolerance. It's a reminder that disagreements are natural among diverse individuals and that it's more productive to recognize and respect differences rather than perpetually contest them. It's about prioritizing relationships and mutual respect over the need to be "right."

The Two Chefs' Culinary Clash

In the heart of Florence, the city synonymous with art and taste, there stood "Bella Cucina," an enchanting bistro known far and wide for its culinary wonders. The kitchen was a stage, and the chefs, the stars of the show. At its helm were Chef Antonio, a stout man with silver hair and eyes that spoke of a thousand recipes, and Chef Marco, young, lanky, with a fire in his eyes that was, more often than not, directed at Antonio.

You see, Antonio was a traditionalist. "The sauce," he'd often proclaim, "must simmer for hours to achieve its rich flavor." His hands moved with grace and precision, like a painter on canvas, as he adhered strictly to age-old recipes passed down through generations.

Marco, on the other hand, was a maverick. "Innovation," he'd retort, "is the soul of modern cuisine!" His dishes, often a juxtaposition of flavors and textures, were testament to his belief in bending rules.

One particular day, the bistro was abuzz with anticipation. A renowned food critic was expected, and the air was thick with tension. A clash was imminent. The duo, in their quest to outdo the other, almost set the kitchen on fire. A basil leaf short of disaster, a bowl of risotto was flung across the room, landing with a splat.

Enough was enough. Rosa, the age-old waitress who had been with "Bella Cucina" since its inception, intervened. "Both of you, out!" she ordered, pointing at the small courtyard. The chefs, albeit reluctantly, obeyed.

Under the Tuscan sun, amidst olive trees and the distant hum of the city, Marco burst out, "Your methods are outdated, Antonio! We need to evolve!"

Antonio shot back, "Tradition is the backbone of our cuisine. You can't just change things on a whim!"

The heated debate continued, the air filled with mentions of sauces, spices, and techniques, until Rosa, her patience wearing thin, exclaimed, "Enough!"

Both chefs turned to her, a bit taken aback by her assertiveness.

"Look at you both," she sighed. "Passionate, yes. But constantly at loggerheads. Why not understand that both of you have a place in this kitchen? Antonio, with his cherished traditions, and Marco, with his fearless innovations."

The chefs looked at each other, the realization slowly dawning upon them. Their constant tug of war was neither productive nor pleasant.

Finally, it was Marco who broke the silence, extending a hand towards Antonio, "Let's agree that we don't agree. But together, we make 'Bella Cucina' what it is."

Antonio, after a moment's hesitation, grasped the offered hand, "Agreed."

From that day forth, "Bella Cucina" saw harmonious collaborations between old and new. Some dishes bore the mark of Antonio's traditional touch, while others sang of Marco's innovative spirit. And some, a beautiful blend of both.

The tale of "The Two Chefs' Culinary Clash" is more than a mere kitchen quarrel. It's a reminder that differing opinions aren't barriers, but opportunities. For growth, for learning, for creating something truly magical. It's about understanding that it's okay to not always see eye to eye, as long as we respect and acknowledge the value each perspective brings. The peace pact they formed wasn't just about their dishes; it was about life itself.

6.2 Navigating Indecisions: "I don't know always means no."

The sentence "I don't know always means no." encapsulates a perspective on decision-making, suggesting that if one is unsure or ambivalent about a decision, it may be wiser to lean towards a negative response, or at the very least, hold off on committing until more clarity is achieved.

In navigating indecision, this sentiment acknowledges a few key aspects:

1. **Protection from Hasty Choices**: Often, "I don't know" is an instinctual or gut response when something doesn't feel right but we can't articulate why. By interpreting it as a "no," we allow ourselves the protection from potentially harmful or premature decisions.

2. **Significance of Certainty**: For some decisions, being sure is crucial. Think about relationships, career changes, or significant financial decisions. If your immediate feeling isn't enthusiasm or assurance, treating "I don't know" as "no" can be a safeguard until you're sure, one way or another.

3. **Eliminates Paralysis by Analysis**: Sometimes, we overthink decisions, waiting for the perfect choice to become clear. If "I don't know" defaults to "no," it can provide a momentary respite from this cycle, allowing for a clearer evaluation of the situation.

4. **Time as an Ally**: Treating "I don't know" as "no" doesn't mean it's a permanent decision. Instead, it

can mean taking more time to reflect, gather information, or simply wait for personal feelings to become clearer.

5. **Encourages Authenticity**: It promotes honest communication with oneself. If you're not wholeheartedly into something or have reservations, it's okay to step back.

6. **Respect for Intuition**: Our instincts often pick up on nuances that our conscious mind overlooks. "I don't know" might be a subtle hint from our subconscious, signaling that something's off or not aligned with our values or current life situation.

In essence, interpreting "I don't know" as "no" when navigating indecision is about self-preservation, patience, and respect for one's own intuition and timing. It's a reminder that it's okay not to rush, that it's okay to wait for clarity, and that sometimes, the absence of a clear "yes" is a clear answer in itself.

Anna's Multiple Choice Dilemma

The sun was setting, casting a warm amber hue over the quaint little cafe where Anna sat, surrounded by the soft hum of chatter and the aroma of roasted coffee beans. She was faced with a menu, each item looking as tantalizing as the next. Caramel macchiato, hazelnut latte, mocha frappe - a symphony of choices, each with its own seductive allure.

And yet, Anna hesitated.

For most people, this might seem like a fleeting, inconsequential moment. But for Anna, this was a reflection of her life's larger quandaries. From choosing her college major, picking a city to call home, to even deciding on relationships - Anna was perpetually caught in the snare of indecision.

"I don't know," she'd often sigh, her voice laced with exasperation, whether discussing her future career or her coffee selection.

Beside her sat Maya, her childhood friend. Maya, with her piercing blue eyes and no-nonsense demeanor, was always one for clarity. "Anna," she said, leaning forward, "when you can't decide, when everything becomes an 'I don't know', it's the universe telling you it's a 'no'."

Anna raised an eyebrow, the whirlwind of choices momentarily forgotten. "So, you're saying that my indecision, this...fence-sitting I always do, means I should just say no?"

Maya chuckled, taking a sip from her cup. "Think of it this way: indecision is like static on a radio. When the channel isn't clear, it's better to switch off or change the station. 'I don't know' is your static, and when you hear it, maybe it's best to move on until the signal is clear."

Anna's fingers traced the rim of her cup, lost in thought. She thought about all the times she had been stuck, unable to move forward because of her indecision. The internships she missed, the relationships she couldn't commit to, the experiences she let slip by. Was it all because she was waiting for a clear 'yes' that never came?

With a newfound determination, she looked up at the barista, "I'll have a plain black coffee, thank you." Simple, clear, devoid of any frills - just like her new approach to life.

As the steam from her cup curled into the evening air, Anna realized that sometimes, not knowing is an answer in itself. And in the cacophony of life's endless choices, it's okay to seek simplicity, to recognize the 'static', and to say 'no' when the heart whispers, "I don't know."

The next time you find yourself on the precipice of indecision, think of Anna and the quiet cafe. Remember that 'I don't know' might just be the universe's gentle nudge towards a clearer, more resonant 'yes' elsewhere.

Lessons

From the story of **Anna's Multiple Choice Dilemma**, we can extract several valuable lessons:

1. **Indecision as a Sign:** Continual indecision or uncertainty about a choice may be an indication that it's not the right one. If something truly aligns with our desires or needs, it will often feel clearer.

2. **Simplicity Amidst Complexity:** Sometimes, amidst a world full of complex choices and overwhelming options, it's okay to choose simplicity. Not every decision needs layers and frills.

3. **The Static Analogy:** Much like a radio searching for a clear signal amidst the static, our minds, too, seek clarity. Recognizing the 'static' in our lives can guide us towards decisions that resonate more deeply with us.

4. **External Perspectives:** Having a trusted confidant, like Maya for Anna, can provide invaluable insights. Sometimes, a fresh perspective can make things clearer or provide a different angle we hadn't considered.

5. **Missed Opportunities:** Indecision can lead to missed opportunities. It's crucial to discern when to wait for clarity and when to make a choice, even if it's just to learn from it.

6. **Embracing Simplicity:** In an era of abundance and endless choices, there's strength in embracing the basic, unadulterated experiences that often bring us the most satisfaction.
7. **Trust in the Universe:** Sometimes, it's essential to trust that the universe has its way of nudging us in the right direction. What might seem like confusion might be a sign to redirect our path.
8. **Inner Resonance:** True alignment with a decision often comes from a place of inner resonance, a gut feeling, or an intuitive 'knowing'. If we constantly feel uncertain, it might be a sign that we're not truly aligned with that particular choice.

In essence, Anna's story serves as a reminder that while life presents us with a multitude of choices, it's essential to tune into our inner selves, recognize the 'static', and be courageous enough to either wait for clarity or move in a direction that feels right.

Chapter 7: Defending Personal Boundaries

Imagine, for a moment, a garden. Your garden. Each plant is lovingly chosen, each petal, a reflection of a part of you. The vibrant tulips mirror your joys; the resilient cacti, your strength through hardships; and the delicate orchids, your most intimate dreams and fears. This garden is yours, and its every detail tells your story.

Now, picture a fence around this garden. Not a prison wall, but a gentle boundary. It safeguards the sanctity of what's inside. Just like this fence, personal boundaries are your invisible shields. They don't trap you; they protect you.

"Hey! Mind if I pick a few flowers for my vase?" a neighbor asks, reaching over the fence. You pause. It's a simple request. But these aren't just flowers. They are fragments of you.

You might think, "It's just a few flowers. What's the harm?" But today's few flowers can become tomorrow's trampled bed of roses if we're not careful. And it's here that the beauty and necessity of defending our personal boundaries shimmer brightly.

Boundaries aren't about keeping people out; they're about valuing what's inside. It's not selfish to protect what matters to you. In fact, it's essential. When boundaries are porous, you risk diluting your essence, letting external influences sway your internal compass.

Yet, stating boundaries is no walk in the park. It requires courage. You might falter, thinking, "What would they say?" But remember, it's your garden, your sanctuary. And while it's okay to share its beauty, it's equally okay to say, "I'd rather you didn't pluck the flowers."

In an age where over-sharing and hyper-connectivity are the norms, defending these doors might seem anachronistic. But it's more vital than ever. These boundaries aren't mere physical or emotional barriers; they are a declaration of self-respect, an affirmation that we value our mental and emotional well-being.

But why is it essential to defend these boundaries?

1. **Preservation of Self**: Just as a pearl remains pristine inside its shell, away from external pollutants, our core self needs protection. Boundaries ensure that while we interact with the world, our fundamental nature remains unaltered.

2. **Avoiding Emotional Drain**: Continual exposure to external demands can be emotionally exhausting. A firm boundary acts as a filter, allowing us to engage with the world on our own terms, conserving our emotional energy.

3. **Ensuring Mental Clarity**: With boundaries, we can better control the influx of external information, opinions, and demands, ensuring our mental space remains uncluttered. This clarity is invaluable, helping us make informed and balanced decisions.

However, setting and maintaining boundaries isn't without its challenges. There's the fear of being labeled 'selfish' or 'aloof.' There's the discomfort of potential confrontation. But herein lies the beauty of boundaries: they teach us the art of graceful assertion. To say 'no' without guilt, to prioritize oneself without apology.

In essence, defending personal boundaries isn't about shutting the world out. It's about celebrating oneself. It's an ode to our worth, a testament to our autonomy, and a salute to our resilience.

So, the next time you feel a twinge of unease, a niggling doubt, or a sense of being overwhelmed, take a moment. Reflect. Maybe it's not about what's coming in, but about the doors you've left ajar. Adjust them, fortify them, and stand by them. For in defending your boundaries, you're not just carving out a space for yourself in the world; you're also sculpting a world that respects and values you in return.

7.1 Standing Firm: "I'm sorry if I gave the impression that you can talk to me like this."

Imagine, if you will, a quiet stream. Its waters are calm and inviting, gently flowing towards the vast ocean. Over time, many travelers, upon discovering this serene waterway, dip their feet in to savor its tranquility, but a few, mistaking its quietude for submission, throw in stones, disrupting its peace.

Such is the essence of the statement, "I'm sorry if I gave the impression that you can talk to me like this."

This phrase is not a manifestation of weakness, nor is it an apology rooted in guilt. It's a gentle yet firm reclamation of respect. A declaration that one's kindness or patience shouldn't be mistaken for vulnerability or a lack of self-worth. In essence, it's a reminder of the human dignity we all inherently possess and should uphold.

There's a grace in these words, a nuanced dance between vulnerability and strength. On the surface, it begins with "I'm sorry," suggesting a hint of regret. But this regret is not for oneself, but rather for any misunderstanding that might've allowed someone else to overstep a boundary. The rest of the sentence firmly and unequivocally establishes that boundary.

In life, it's natural to encounter individuals who might mistake one's open-heartedness for an open invitation to take liberties. There are those who perceive patience as passivity, understanding as endorsement, or empathy as endorsement of their actions, words, or behaviors. And in these moments, this statement becomes more than just words – it's a shield, a line drawn in the sand, signaling that respect is non-negotiable.

But beyond the immediate message to the perpetrator, this statement speaks volumes to oneself. It reaffirms one's self-worth, asserting that every individual deserves respect, irrespective of their demeanor, past interactions, or societal perceptions.

The next time you imagine that tranquil stream, let it be a reminder. Its serenity is its strength. It accommodates, it nurtures, but it demands respect. And like that stream, with this statement, one asserts that while they might flow with grace and patience, they have the strength to stand against those who wish to disrupt their peace.

Daniel's Encounter at the Café

The sun streamed in, casting lazy shadows on the cobblestone streets. The scent of roasted coffee beans wafted through the air, filling the café with an intoxicating aroma. The café, "Le Soleil", was a mosaic of life – old men playing chess, lovers whispering sweet nothings, a writer lost in the depths of his novel, and Daniel, waiting.

With a steaming cup of cappuccino in hand, he settled at a corner table, engrossed in a book. Every so often, he'd pause, allowing the words to seep into his consciousness, and then he'd lose himself again in the labyrinth of sentences. The world around him faded, but not for long.

"Hey! Haven't seen you in a while!" boomed a voice, breaking his reverie. It was Ben, a distant acquaintance from college, with a personality as loud as his voice. Before Daniel could even greet him, Ben plonked himself down across the table, his eyes scanning Daniel, almost judgmental. "Still reading these kinds of books? No wonder you were always a bit...you know," he chuckled, hinting at something Daniel knew all too well.

The memories from college came rushing back: days when Daniel felt overwhelmed, days when words seemed too heavy, and days when Ben's teasing bordered on cruelty. But that was the past. Today, he was different.

As Ben continued to jest and jibe, Daniel took a deep breath, feeling the weight of the moment. "Ben," Daniel began, pausing for effect, "I'm sorry if I gave the impression that you can talk to me like this." There was no anger, just a firm, unwavering assertion of self-respect. The café seemed to go silent for a heartbeat.

Ben, taken aback, blinked a few times, clearly not expecting such a retort. The jest in his eyes replaced with surprise. "I...I was just..." he stammered, searching for words. But before he could finish, Daniel, with a small smile, added, "It's good to see you, Ben. I hope you're well." And with that, he returned to his book, sipping his cappuccino.

In that fleeting moment, amid the clatter of coffee cups and murmured conversations, Daniel wasn't just standing up to Ben. He was standing up for every voice that had ever been silenced, every soul that had ever been belittled. He was standing firm.

Ben shifted uncomfortably, casting a fleeting glance at the other patrons, wondering if they had overheard the exchange. The jovial, dominating air he carried seemed to dissipate. "Look, Danny," he began, attempting familiarity, "I was just joking around, like old times."

But Daniel, looking up from his book, held Ben's gaze steadily. "Times change, Ben. So do people," he said calmly, the layers of growth and experience evident in his tone.

Ben, fumbling with his words, tried to save face. "You've always been too sensitive. It's just banter, man."

"You see," Daniel replied, leaning slightly forward, drawing Ben into his space, "it's all about boundaries. Just as you choose to express yourself freely, I choose how I'm treated. There's no harm in recalling the past, but living there? That's where we differ."

The weight of the silence that followed was palpable. Daniel's words, simple yet profound, resonated deeply within the confines of the quaint café. The old men playing chess threw sidelong glances, the lovers whispered even lower, and the writer scribbled away furiously, perhaps capturing the essence of the moment.

Ben, never having been at a loss for words, was silent. The confident, boisterous college mate Daniel once knew was now grappling with an unfamiliar emotion: introspection.

After what felt like an eternity, Ben cleared his throat, looking genuinely apologetic. "I guess I got carried away, thinking about the old days. I'm sorry, Danny."

Daniel's smile was genuine as he nodded. "That's all we ever need, Ben: understanding and growth."

The two parted ways, one returning to his world of words, the other stepping out into the sunlit streets with a newfound respect and introspection. The café, "Le

Soleil", once again became a mosaic of life, but this time with a story of its own: a tale of boundaries, self-worth, and the eternal dance of words.

Lessons

The story of "Daniel's Encounter at the Café" imparts several valuable lessons:

1. **Self-Respect is Paramount:** Regardless of our past experiences or relationships, it's essential to maintain a strong sense of self-worth and demand the respect we deserve. Just because someone was once part of our journey does not grant them the right to belittle or mock us, especially if it crosses our personal boundaries.

2. **Growth is Inevitable:** People change and evolve. The person we knew or were in the past isn't necessarily who we are today. Recognizing and honoring that growth is crucial for both self and in our interactions with others.

3. **Communication is Key:** It's not just about standing up for oneself; it's about how we do it. Daniel's calm, firm, and composed manner of addressing Ben's jabs highlights the power of mature communication.

4. **Boundaries are Essential:** Every individual has their personal boundaries, and these should be respected. It's okay to assert them and let others know when they've crossed a line.

5. **Introspection Leads to Growth:** Just as Daniel had grown over the years, the story nudges Ben—and by extension, the reader—towards introspection. Recognizing our missteps and genuinely attempting to understand and correct them is a sign of personal growth.
6. **Simplicity Holds Power:** Sometimes, the most impactful messages aren't shouted but whispered. Simple statements, when delivered with conviction, can resonate deeply and leave a lasting impression.

In essence, the story is a gentle yet profound reminder of the importance of self-worth, boundaries, and the continuous journey of personal growth. It underscores the idea that respect isn't just something we demand but something we deserve, in all phases and places of life.

7.2 The Intuition Guide: "It all sounds logical, but my gut tells me otherwise."

The realm of decision-making is vast, often spread across the landscapes of reason and emotion. When we talk about "The Intuition Guide," we are essentially discussing that innate, inner compass—a guiding light that often surfaces in moments of indecision. It's a whisper, a sensation, a 'feeling' that may not always align with what appears logical on paper. The sentence, "It all sounds logical, but my gut tells me otherwise," encapsulates this delicate dance between cognition and intuition.

1. The Dominance of Logic:

We're educated to value the power of logic, aren't we? From school to workplaces, there's a continuous emphasis on structured thinking, reasoning, and data-driven decisions. For every problem, we're trained to find a solution based on evidence and facts. It's about linear paths, structured solutions, and the conscious processing of available information.

2. The Undercurrent of Intuition:

Contrary to logic, intuition operates subconsciously. It's not about step-by-step processing; instead, it encapsulates our experiences, inherent knowledge, and subconscious observations. Intuition is like the background app that's always running, absorbing patterns and nuances that our conscious self might overlook. It's that sudden 'knowing' we feel even when we don't have all the facts.

3. The Intersection of the Two:
The sentence "It all sounds logical, but my gut tells me otherwise" highlights a critical juncture where logic and intuition meet. It signifies a situation where, despite all the logical reasoning pointing one way, there's an inner voice suggesting another direction. This is the Intuition Guide in action. It's a gentle nudge, a reminder to pause and reassess. It does not discredit logic but asks for a more holistic approach to decision-making, one that encompasses both the cerebral and the visceral.

4. Why Listen to The Intuition Guide?
The Intuition Guide, embodied in that single sentence, serves as a protection mechanism. Humans have evolved with intuition as a means of survival. When our ancestors sensed danger in the wilderness, they often didn't have the luxury of time to analyze the situation logically. They relied on their gut feelings, which were the result of accumulated knowledge and experiences. In today's world, while the dangers have evolved, the mechanism remains relevant. From making business decisions to choosing life partners, sometimes our gut instinct catches what our logical mind misses.

5. Embracing the Balance:
To navigate life effectively, we must understand that neither logic nor intuition should be exclusively relied

upon. They are not opposing forces but complementary tools. Embracing both allows for a comprehensive decision-making approach.

In essence, "The Intuition Guide" and the sentiment "It all sounds logical, but my gut tells me otherwise" champions the idea of harmonizing the power of reason with the depth of instinct. In a world that's increasingly complex, it serves as a reminder that sometimes, the answers aren't just in the data, the facts, or the apparent logic. Sometimes, they reside deep within us, waiting for us to listen, trust, and act.

Rachel's Crossroads

The sun was setting in its gentle amber hues, painting the sky in warm pastels. Rachel found herself at the heart of Crossroads Town - an aptly named place for someone entangled in the web of her own life's decisions.

Now, Rachel was a mathematician. Logic and reason were her closest allies. Her days consisted of numbers, equations, and proofs. She dealt with absolutes; there were right answers and wrong ones. In her world, ambiguity was the enemy.

On this particular evening, she faced a quandary not solvable by mere calculations. The town's council presented a seemingly perfect plan for urban development. It promised economic growth, better housing, and amenities. Everything, on paper, was faultless. It was the sort of proposition that didn't just make sense—it screamed sense.

But something gnawed at Rachel's insides. A subtle, inexplicable tug, pulling her away from the clean numbers and logical arguments. "It all sounds logical," she whispered to herself, eyes squinting as if hoping to discern truth from the twilight, "but my gut tells me otherwise."

She recollected tales her grandmother told her, stories of intuition, of the heart's silent whispers often drowned in the cacophony of reason. She remembered one tale vividly: a sailor who changed his planned course not because of the weather forecast but because of a dream. That very night, a storm ravaged his initial path. It wasn't logic; it was a deep, ancient understanding, an intuition.

Her grandmother's words echoed, "Sometimes, dear, our gut is the compass we forget we have."

Rachel decided to delve deeper. She met with old town residents, heard their stories, and learned about the legacy of Crossroads Town—a legacy not visible in numbers but felt in heartbeats, shared laughter, and timeless memories. The town wasn't just buildings and roads; it was stories, histories, and lives intertwined.

Two weeks later, she presented a new proposal to the council, one that preserved the town's essence while embracing growth. It was met with a few raised eyebrows but ultimately, admiration and agreement.

Rachel's decision wasn't just a victory for Crossroads Town but for every silent voice within us that urges us to listen, to feel beyond the obvious. For in the dance between logic and intuition, there's a rhythm, a balance. Rachel's journey was not against reason but a plea for the heart's voice to be heard amidst the logical symphony.

In life's numerous crossroads, let Rachel's tale be a gentle reminder: Sometimes, the loudest answers are those whispered softly by our soul.

Lessons

From Rachel's poignant journey at the crossroads of decision-making, several lessons emerge:

1. **Trust Your Gut**: Even in a world dominated by facts, data, and logical reasoning, there's value in listening to our intuition. Our subconscious picks up on nuances that our conscious mind might overlook.

2. **Balance is Key**: While logic and reason are essential, so are emotions and instincts. Striking a balance between the two can lead to more holistic and considerate decisions.

3. **Legacy Matters**: Development and progress are crucial, but not at the expense of erasing history, culture, and the emotional bonds people share with a place.

4. **Deep Listening**: Beyond numbers and surface narratives lie stories, emotions, and legacies. Truly listening can uncover insights that might be missed otherwise.

5. **Courage to Challenge the Norm**: Just because something appears perfect on paper doesn't mean it's the best course of action. It takes courage to challenge popular opinion based on a personal, intuitive understanding.

6. **Value of Personal Stories**: Every individual, every community has a story. These narratives can offer

invaluable insights and should be considered in decision-making processes.

7. **Embrace Both Heart and Mind**: Rachel's journey emphasizes that the best decisions often come from a place where the heart and mind meet, each informing the other.

In essence, Rachel's story is a testament to the intricate dance between logic and emotion, urging us to not just think but also to feel our way through life's myriad choices.

Chapter 8: Cherishing Time and Priorities

Time is one of the few constants in our lives, an ever-ticking metronome that measures our existence in heartbeats, sunrises, and fleeting moments. Yet, its very constancy often blinds us to its value. We're surrounded by the narrative that "time is money," but in truth, time is far more precious, for while money can often be recouped, time, once spent, remains an irretrievable gift.

When we talk about cherishing time, we delve into the depths of mindfulness—of being present and fully experiencing each moment. To cherish is to hold something dear, to recognize its value and treat it with care. When applied to time, this means appreciating the ephemeral nature of moments and being intentional about how we spend them.

However, our relationship with time isn't as straightforward as one might think. Without a lens through which to view it, time can become a blurred rush of moments. This is where priorities enter the discussion. Priorities act as that lens, providing clarity and focus. They guide us, helping us decide where to invest our time and ensuring that it aligns with our values and aspirations.

Priorities are individualistic. For one person, prioritizing family might mean spending evenings and weekends at home, while for another, it could be about securing a future through long hours of work. But it's the act of prioritization, the conscious choice, that turns time from a mere resource into a treasure trove of meaningful experiences.

In the vast mosaic of existence, where moments are the tesserae, priorities act as the artist's hand, guiding each piece into its place, ensuring that the overall picture is not just coherent but beautiful. When we prioritize, we're not merely organizing our lives; we're sculpting them.

Yet, it's essential to recognize that priorities aren't static. They shift and evolve with life's changing seasons. The key is regular introspection, ensuring that our time aligns with what we currently hold dear. It's a dance between the heart and the clock, between desires and hours.

In conclusion, to cherish time is not just to count it, but to make it count. It's about quality over quantity, moments over minutes. When combined with well-defined priorities, time becomes more than just the backdrop of our lives; it transforms into the medium through which we paint our masterpiece. So, as we move through the gallery of life, let's ensure that each canvas, each day, reflects not just the passing of time, but the artistry of intention, passion, and purpose.

8.1 Valuing Moments: "I don't want to take the time for that now."

Time, in its very nature, is a paradox. It's abundant yet finite, a resource we all possess, yet no one can truly own. At its core, time is the continuum on which the human experience is played out, and every moment, a fleeting episode within that narrative. However, not all moments carry the same weight, and therein lies the art of prioritization and cherishing time.

The phrase, "I don't want to take the time for that now," isn't about rejection or avoidance, but rather a deep-rooted assertion of value. It signals an intimate understanding of one's own temporal currency and the inherent worth of the activities and experiences it can purchase.

Imagine, for a moment, a scale. On one side, you have the inexhaustible, ever-ticking minutes of your life. On the other, you have the multitude of activities, tasks, and experiences vying for those minutes. To "cherish" time is to strike a balance, ensuring that what you place on the latter does justice to the former.

This statement also underscores the importance of mindfulness and presence. The modern world is a cacophony of distractions, demands, and desires. Amidst this whirlwind, it's easy to lose oneself, scattering time across a myriad of tasks that might seem urgent but aren't necessarily important. By saying, "I don't want to take the time for that now," we ground ourselves in the present, making a conscious choice to engage with what truly resonates with our values and aspirations.

Furthermore, it's a gentle reminder that time, once given, cannot be reclaimed. A moment spent is a moment gone. Therefore, when we decide where to allocate our time, we're not just making logistical choices; we're curating our life story. It's akin to an artist selecting which hues to add to a painting, considering not just the immediate impact but the long-term composition.

Lastly, it's pivotal to remember that this isn't just about grand gestures or significant life events. The beauty of cherishing time often lies in the mundane, the everyday moments that, when strung together, form the essence of our existence. It could be as simple as deciding to watch a sunset over completing a task or choosing to listen to a friend over mindlessly scrolling through a social feed.

In conclusion, "I don't want to take the time for that now" is a powerful testament to the art of living intentionally. It encourages us to be custodians of our own time, to cherish it, prioritize it, and most importantly, to invest it in moments that truly matter. Because while the sands of time never cease, with awareness and intention, we can craft a journey that's both meaningful and memorable.

Tim's Day of Choices

The sun crept over the horizon, spreading a warm tangerine hue across Tim's bedroom wall. He blinked open his eyes and, for a brief moment, just listened to the world outside. Birds sang, distant cars hummed, and the aroma of fresh coffee wafted in. The day lay stretched out in front of him, a canvas of endless opportunities.

That's when his phone buzzed, an interruption in his tranquil moment. A notification blinked - a friend's invitation to a brunch in the city, a two-hour drive away. Tim paused. The old Tim would've rushed, showered, dressed, and embarked on that long drive without a second thought. But today was different.

"I don't want to take the time for that now," he whispered to himself, taking a moment to relish the weight of the sentence, the affirmation of his own priorities.

Instead, he walked into the kitchen and began to make his breakfast. He cherished the sizzle of eggs, the warm embrace of toast, and the simple joy of morning radio. Each bite was an event, each sound an orchestra, each scent a fond memory.

In the afternoon, as sunbeams danced lazily around his living room, Tim faced another choice. He could dive into the rabbit hole of social media, a world of curated lives and endless scrolling, or he could take a leisurely walk in the park. Once again, he chose the latter. The chirping of crickets, the rustling of leaves underfoot, and the gentle caress of the wind became his companions. He felt alive, present, connected.

By evening, when the skies painted themselves in shades of lavender and gold, another buzz beckoned. An invitation to a webinar, promising secrets of productivity. But Tim, lounging with a book by the fireplace, gently declined. "I don't want to take the time for that now."

As stars took their place in the vast canvas of the night, Tim reflected on his choices. He hadn't done anything extraordinary. There was no thrilling adventure or significant achievement. But there was contentment, peace, and a deep connection to the present.

For sometimes, the bravest choice is choosing what we won't do, so we can fully immerse in what we truly wish to. And as the quiet night embraced the world, Tim knew he had made the right choices, cherishing moments over mere motions.

Lessons

From the story "Tim's Day of Choices," several poignant lessons emerge:

1. **The Power of Pause:** In a world that constantly pushes us to move faster, there's immense value in taking a moment to pause, reflect, and decide what truly aligns with our priorities.

2. **Valuing Simplicity:** Extravagance and adventure have their moments, but there's unparalleled beauty in simple pleasures — the sizzle of eggs, a walk in the park, or reading by the fireplace. Sometimes, simplicity offers a deeper, more profound satisfaction.

3. **Embracing the Present:** Being fully present allows us to experience life more deeply. Whether it's savoring a meal or feeling the wind on a walk, mindfulness enhances our experiences.

4. **Affirmation of Priorities:** It's okay to say no. By prioritizing what matters most to us, we're not missing out — we're making conscious choices that resonate with our authentic selves.

5. **Connection Over Distraction:** In a digital age, it's easy to get lost in endless scrolling or be constantly connected. Yet, disconnecting occasionally allows us to form genuine connections with our surroundings and ourselves.

6. **The Luxury of Choice:** Every day presents us with countless choices. Recognizing that we have the agency to choose allows us to live life more intentionally.

7. **Quality Over Quantity:** It's not about how much we do, but the depth and quality of our experiences. A

day spent with intention and presence can be far more fulfilling than a packed schedule.

8. **Contentment in Choices:** True contentment doesn't come from external validations or achievements, but from aligning our actions with our inner values.

Through Tim's day, we're reminded that every moment holds choices, and these choices shape the richness of our lives. Making decisions that align with our core values, even if they seem simple or mundane, can lead to a deeper sense of satisfaction and fulfillment.

8.2 Embracing Change: "I changed my mind."

Change, in all its forms and flavors, is the very essence of life. The world around us perpetually evolves — seasons change, civilizations rise and fall, and the universe itself is in a constant state of expansion. Amidst this grand dance of transformation, human beings, with their intricate tapestry of emotions, thoughts, and willpower, are no exception.

The phrase "I changed my mind" is simple, yet it holds within it a universe of evolution, realization, and personal growth. Let's unpack the profound depth embedded within this declaration:

1. **Admission of Growth:** When someone admits they've changed their mind, they're essentially acknowledging personal growth. It implies that they've encountered new information or experiences that reshaped their perspective.

2. **Flexibility in Thought:** Rigidity in beliefs and ideas can stifle progress. Changing one's mind demonstrates an adaptability and openness to new concepts, suggesting a mind that's fluid and receptive.

3. **Courage to Admit Alteration:** In many societies, changing one's stance or viewpoint can be seen as a sign of weakness. Thus, openly stating "I changed my mind" requires a certain bravery, as it defies the societal expectation to always be steadfast.

4. **Valuing Experience over Ego:** It's all too easy to cling to an idea simply because admitting change

would mean conceding that one's previous belief might have been flawed. When someone says they've changed their mind, they prioritize personal growth and understanding over their ego.

5. **The Impermanence of Life:** Nothing in life is static. Just as rivers meander and mountains erode, human thought processes are in a state of flux. Recognizing and embracing this change mirrors the transient nature of existence.

6. **The Freedom of Choice:** Every individual has the autonomy to revise their beliefs and decisions. "I changed my mind" is an assertion of this personal freedom, a reminder that we are not bound by our past decisions or beliefs.

7. **Embracing Uncertainty:** Changing one's mind often comes after periods of doubt and introspection. It showcases the acceptance of uncertainty in life, understanding that absolute clarity is rare, and it's okay to pivot when faced with ambiguity.

In essence, "I changed my mind" is not just a shift in perspective but a testament to human resilience and adaptability. It celebrates the continuous journey of learning, unlearning, and relearning. Embracing change, both externally and within, allows for a fuller, richer experience of life, for it is in the ebb and flow of beliefs, in the dance of thoughts, that we truly come alive. It's a reminder that change, in all its unpredictability, is not a detour in our journey but the journey itself.

Alice's U-turn Decision

Sun-kissed mornings in Willowville were a sight to behold, with golden hues painting every corner, and the promise of a new day lingering in the air. It was on such a day, not too long ago, that Alice stood at the threshold of the town's acclaimed institute, ready to embark on a journey she had meticulously charted out.

Young, driven, and with a heart full of dreams, Alice had her life planned to the T. From being the school topper to securing the much-coveted seat at Willowville Institute of Technology, she had always been on the fast track to success. People envied her clarity and determination. After all, here was a girl who knew exactly where she was going.

But sometimes, life has a curious way of unravelling our certainties.

Midway through her first semester, Alice found herself sitting in the ancient, oak-paneled library, surrounded by a fortress of books, yet feeling utterly lost. The algorithms and theories that once intrigued her now seemed lifeless and mundane. The more she tried to fit into the mold she had cast for herself, the more she felt like a square peg in a round hole.

One evening, as the golden sunset hues streamed through the tall library windows, Alice stumbled upon an old, worn-out book on Renaissance Art. Each page, filled with vibrant frescoes and poetic verses, breathed life. The profound strokes of Da Vinci, the passionate hues of Michelangelo, all spoke to her, evoking emotions she had forgotten.

Days turned into weeks, and Alice found herself spending more hours in the arts section, sketching on margins, writing verses, and feeling alive. The realization was slow yet profound. She was in love with art, with its chaos, its rawness, and its boundless freedom.

It wasn't easy, the day Alice stood up in front of her peers and professors, announcing, "I changed my mind." She felt a mix of anxiety and liberation. There were whispers, some of confusion and others of admiration. But Alice, for the first time, felt in sync with herself.

She transferred to Florence, the heart of the Renaissance, trading microprocessors for Michelangelo, algorithms for art. In the cobblestone streets and historic piazzas, Alice found her calling. Her sketches brought to life the tales of the city, and her verses echoed its soul.

Years later, as she showcased her work in a grand gallery, Alice fondly remembered that pivotal moment in Willowville. The U-turn wasn't a deviation but a homecoming. It was a testament to the world, and more so to herself, that it's never too late to embrace change, to listen to one's heart, to take that daunting yet exhilarating U-turn.

Because, in the end, it's not about the road taken but the journey enjoyed.

Chapter 9: Delving into Relationships and Authenticity

Relationships are like gardens. They need time, effort, and the right ingredients to flourish. When we think about the people close to us, like friends or family, it's important to understand how being real, or authentic, plays a big role in making those bonds strong.

So, what does it mean to be authentic in relationships?

Imagine a friend who always says "yes" even when they want to say "no", or someone who pretends to like something just because everyone else does. Over time, these little pretenses add up, and that friend may feel tired, stressed, or even disconnected from those around them. This is where authenticity comes in.

Being authentic means showing our true selves. It's like taking off a mask and letting others see the real us, with our strengths, weaknesses, likes, and dislikes. It's about being honest with how we feel and what we think.

But why is this so important in relationships?

- **Trust**: When we're genuine, people trust us more. They know we're not hiding anything and that our words match our actions.

- **Understanding**: Being true to ourselves helps others understand us better. They get to know our real likes and dislikes, what makes us happy, and what upsets us.

- **Deep Connections**: Authenticity allows for deeper connections. When we're open about who we are, it encourages others to do the same, making conversations and time together more meaningful.

- **Less Stress**: Pretending is exhausting! Being real means, we don't have to remember all the things we've said or done to fit in.

However, being authentic doesn't mean we should be rude or say everything that comes to mind. It's about being true to ourselves while also being kind and considerate of others.

In the end, true relationships are built on honesty, respect, and love. When we bring our genuine selves into our relationships, we create a space where everyone feels seen, heard, and valued. And just like a well-tended garden, these relationships bloom into something beautiful and lasting.

9.1 Recognizing Mismatches: "We just don't fit together."

Imagine you have a puzzle. Each piece has its unique shape, and when you try to fit two pieces together, they either click seamlessly or just don't fit. It's not that there's something wrong with either piece; they're just not made for each other.

The phrase "We just don't fit together" is much like this puzzle analogy. It's about understanding that sometimes, no matter how much we might want something or someone to be a part of our life, they might not be the right fit. And that's okay.

1. Relationships:

Most commonly, we hear this phrase in the context of relationships. It could be friendships, romantic relationships, or even professional partnerships. Sometimes, two people might have different values, beliefs, or goals. Over time, these differences can lead to misunderstandings, conflicts, and feelings of being unfulfilled. Recognizing a mismatch in such situations means understanding that both individuals might be happier and more content apart than together.

2. Personal Values and Surroundings:

Have you ever been in a place—a job, a school, a city—and felt like you don't belong? It might be because your personal values or aspirations don't align with the culture or values of that environment. Recognizing this mismatch is essential for your personal growth and happiness.

3. Goals and Paths:

Sometimes we choose a certain path in life—like a career or a hobby. But as we delve deeper, we realize it's not what we expected or wanted. Recognizing that you've outgrown a certain goal or that it's not fulfilling can help you redirect and find a path more aligned with your desires.

4. Interests and Activities:

We've all been there—joining a club, taking up a sport, or starting a hobby because it sounded fun or because our friends were doing it. But then, it just doesn't feel right. It's not enjoyable. This is a simple case of an interest mismatch.

Recognizing mismatches is all about self-awareness. It's about understanding what feels right and what doesn't. It's essential to remember that acknowledging a mismatch isn't a failure or a negative judgment. It's an understanding that helps us make choices better suited to our happiness and well-being.

In life, it's not about forcing pieces together but finding where they fit naturally. It brings ease, happiness, and genuine connections, be it with people, places, or passions. So, when something feels off, instead of pushing harder, it might be worth stepping back and asking, "Is this a good fit for me?"

Nina and the Incompatible Friend

Nina and Sarah were like two peas in a pod - or at least that's what everyone thought. They met in kindergarten, their fingers smeared with paint as they drew pictures side by side. As the years rolled by, they found themselves stitched together by shared memories: sneaky snacks under the school table, teenage secrets, and joint rebellions against the curfew.

However, as they stepped into their twenties, the world for each began to unfurl differently. Sarah thrived in the hustle and bustle of the city, the cacophony of late-night parties, the jostling crowds at the latest pop-up shops. Nina, on the other hand, sought solace in the quiet embrace of nature, sipped tea at quaint cafes, and roamed the hushed corridors of museums.

While Sarah was planning her next weekend at the newest club in town, Nina was sketching out her next nature retreat. It wasn't that they didn't try to understand each other; it was that their souls were humming different tunes.

One day, over coffee at an old joint they once loved, there was a palpable silence, not the comfortable sort, but the kind that's thick and speaks a thousand words. Nina, ever the introspective one, finally broke it. "Sarah," she began, choosing her words with care, "You know I love you, right? But lately, it feels like we're two jigsaw pieces from different puzzles."

Sarah looked into her mug, the swirling steam reflecting her turmoil. "I've felt it too," she admitted. "I miss us. But, maybe, just maybe, it's not about trying to jam our pieces together anymore."

They both knew the truth in that statement: their worlds had grown apart. It was neither's fault. Time, experiences, and personal growth had simply sculpted them differently.

Their parting wasn't dramatic. No tearful goodbyes, no bitter words. Just an understanding that some paths are meant to diverge. They cherished the memories, the laughter, and the lessons, but also realized the truth of their current situation. Recognizing the mismatch was perhaps the most genuine thing they could do for their friendship.

Years later, they'd sometimes pass each other in the city, offering a smile, a wave, a silent acknowledgment of the bond that once was. Their paths were distinct, but their history was shared, and there's a special kind of beauty in that.

After all, not every story needs to have a 'forever'; some just teach us the value of 'then'. And that's perfectly okay.

Lessons

From the narrative of Nina and Sarah, several insightful lessons emerge:

1. **Growth and Change are Inevitable:** As individuals journey through life, personal growth and evolution are natural. It's crucial to understand that people can change, and their paths can diverge from what was once a shared trajectory.

2. **Acceptance over Resistance:** Instead of resisting change or trying to force relationships to remain the same, acceptance of the present can pave the way for more genuine interactions and peace.

3. **Cherished Memories are Timeless:** Even if relationships change or drift apart, the memories and bonds forged at different times remain precious. They're a testament to moments of connection, joy, and shared experiences.

4. **Mismatch Doesn't Mean Malice:** Recognizing incompatibility doesn't signify any wrongdoing or fault by either party. Sometimes, people grow in different directions, and acknowledging that can be the kindest thing to do.

5. **Silent Acknowledgment is Powerful:** Words aren't always necessary. A simple smile, nod, or gesture can convey a wealth of emotions and shared

history, reinforcing the idea that communication isn't just verbal.

6. **Value of Letting Go:** Holding onto relationships that no longer align with one's growth or values can be more painful than liberating. Letting go, while difficult, can open doors to personal understanding and new experiences.

7. **Every Relationship Has Its Season:** Not every relationship is meant to last a lifetime. Some are short-lived, some last decades, but each has its own season and significance in one's life story.

In essence, the tale of Nina and Sarah underscores the beauty of friendship, the pains of growing apart, and the maturity to recognize and honor both. It serves as a poignant reminder that relationships, much like life, are in constant flux, and that's what makes them so rich and profound.

9.2 Celebrating Self: "At the moment I prefer to meet with myself."

In the ever-evolving dance of life, we often find ourselves swaying to the rhythms of societal expectations, obligations, and the conflict of external voices. We attend gatherings, nod in agreement, mirror emotions, and often blur the lines between our own identities and the masks we wear. But what happens when we decide to tune into our own rhythm, to pause and resonate with our own essence? That's where the profound act of "Celebrating Self" comes into play.

The statement, "At the moment I prefer to meet with myself," is a powerful declaration of self-awareness and self-appreciation. It signifies the realization that one's company, introspection, and self-dialogue can be as enriching, if not more, than any external interaction. It's about understanding that before we can genuinely connect with others, we must first be in sync with ourselves.

Celebrating self is not an act of arrogance or self-indulgence. On the contrary, it's a celebration of one's individuality, emotions, dreams, and vulnerabilities. It's about creating a safe space for our thoughts, taking pride in our strengths, showing compassion for our weaknesses, and understanding our ever-evolving narrative.

In today's hyper-connected world, where FOMO (Fear of Missing Out) is a real phenomenon, choosing to spend time with oneself can be seen as an act of defiance. But it's in these moments of solitude that we cultivate self-love, nurture our passions, and recharge our spirits. Meeting with oneself is akin to touching base with an old friend, where conversations flow freely, memories are revisited, and dreams are rekindled.

Furthermore, celebrating self is about understanding that personal growth often requires personal space. It's about valuing one's mental and emotional well-being over societal norms. It's about realizing that it's okay to decline an invitation, to disconnect, to take a step back, and to journey inwards. Because sometimes, the most meaningful conversations, the most profound revelations, and the most genuine laughter come from those moments when we meet with ourselves.

In essence, "At the moment I prefer to meet with myself," is more than just a statement. It's an invitation to introspection, a celebration of individuality, and most importantly, a gentle reminder that amidst the hustle and bustle of life, we must never lose touch with the person we are at our core.

Oscar's Date with Himself

Oscar's life buzzed with activity. Whether it was catching up with friends at the local pub, engaging in community projects, or bustling between tight work schedules, his calendar was chock-full, each day colored with commitments. To the world, he was the life of the party, always surrounded by friends, always at the center of the buzz.

Yet, one Friday evening, as Oscar sat surrounded by the familiar chatter of his close-knit group of friends, a peculiar feeling washed over him. The conversations around, though filled with laughter and camaraderie, seemed somewhat distant, like a song playing in another room. An unscheduled reflection had crept into Oscar's mind: When was the last time he had truly spent time with himself?

The next morning, on a spontaneous whim, Oscar decided to take himself out on a date. No friends, no work calls, just him. He muted his phone and set out, no destination in mind, guided only by impulse and instinct. The city seemed different, the streets quieter, the air fresher, when he wasn't rushing through it or engrossed in conversation.

He started at a quaint café, ordering his favorite croissant and a cup of coffee. With no one to talk to, Oscar's senses were heightened. He noticed the aroma of freshly ground coffee beans, the soft jazz playing in the background, and the art on the walls he'd always overlooked. With every bite and sip, he was present, savoring the moment.

A walk in the park followed. He watched children play, couples laugh, and birds chirp. He lay on the grass, looking at the vastness of the sky, the drifting clouds mirroring his drifting thoughts. Oscar began to introspect, rekindling memories, dreams, and aspirations that had taken a backseat.

That evening, he found a quiet corner in a bookstore, losing himself in tales of faraway lands and adventures. Later, he treated himself to a meal at a fancy restaurant, not minding the occasional curious glance from couples or groups. To Oscar, the evening was perfect. The meal was a feast not just for his taste buds but his soul.

As the night drew to a close, Oscar sat on his apartment balcony, a warm cup of tea in hand, the city lights painting a serene picture. He felt rejuvenated, having rediscovered parts of himself he'd long forgotten.

It wasn't about solitude or escapism; it was about celebration. Celebrating Oscar, understanding his thoughts, and reigniting his passions. He realized that sometimes the most meaningful conversations are the ones you have with yourself.

From that day on, Oscar made it a ritual. Once a month, he'd say to anyone who asked, "At the moment I prefer to meet with myself." Not as an act of exclusion, but as a celebration of self, because sometimes, in the midst of our busy lives, we all need a date with ourselves.

Lessons

From the story "Oscar's Date with Himself," several valuable lessons can be gleaned:

1. **The Importance of Self-Reflection:** In the midst of our bustling lives, it's crucial to pause and take a moment for introspection. This helps in realigning with our goals, understanding our feelings, and maintaining mental well-being.

2. **Quality Over Quantity:** It's not always about how many engagements or social interactions we have, but the quality of the time spent. A day spent in solitude can sometimes be more fulfilling than numerous social commitments.

3. **Being Present:** Oscar's heightened senses during his solo date emphasize the importance of being present in the moment. Often, we miss out on the little joys because we're either distracted or too preoccupied.

4. **Self-Love and Self-Care:** It's essential to take out time for oneself, to indulge in what makes you happy and relaxed. This isn't selfish; it's necessary for one's emotional and mental health.

5. **Rediscovery:** Spending time alone can lead to the rediscovery of lost passions, dreams, and even

memories. It's an opportunity to reconnect with oneself.

6. **Validation from Within:** Oscar's contentment during his solo date underscores that self-worth and validation should primarily come from within. We don't always need external affirmation to feel valued or content.

7. **Balance in Life:** While social interactions are vital, it's equally important to balance them with moments of solitude, ensuring a holistic approach to well-being.

8. **Breaking Stereotypes:** Oscar's decision to dine alone at a fancy restaurant highlights the importance of breaking societal norms and stereotypes. Doing what feels right for oneself, even if it's unconventional, is vital for personal growth.

9. **Meaningful Conversations:** Sometimes, the most profound and insightful conversations are the ones we have with ourselves. They offer clarity, direction, and understanding.

10. **Routine and Ritual:** Establishing rituals, like Oscar's monthly solo date, can be grounding. They act as anchors, providing stability and predictability in an otherwise chaotic world.

In essence, the story underscores the beauty of solitude, the importance of self-reflection, and the rejuvenation that comes from celebrating oneself.

Chapter 10: Reflecting on Self and Interactions

Our lives are an intricate tapestry of self-awareness and our interactions with the world. Both shape our existence, teaching us about ourselves and the world in which we reside. To lead a fulfilling life, one needs to strike a balance between reflecting on one's self and understanding one's interactions with others.

1.   *Self-Reflection: The   Mirror   Within*
a. **Introspection:** At the core of reflection lies introspection. Delving deep into our thoughts, beliefs, and feelings gives insight into our motivations, desires, and fears. It's a necessary process to understand oneself, make informed decisions, and foster personal growth.

b. **Identifying Strengths and Weaknesses:** Reflecting on one's experiences and actions helps pinpoint areas of strength and aspects that need improvement. Recognizing these areas is the first step towards personal and professional development.

c. **Emotional Intelligence:** Regular self-reflection improves emotional intelligence. Understanding our emotional triggers and responses helps in managing emotions, thereby improving our interactions and relationships.

2.   *The   Dance   of   Interactions*
a. **Understanding Others:** Our interactions with others

act as a window to the larger world. By observing and reflecting on these interactions, we can glean insights into human behavior, societal norms, and cultural dynamics.

b. Feedback Loop: Our interactions often act as feedback mechanisms. They give us a sense of how we're perceived, what we're doing right, and where we might be going astray. This external feedback is invaluable for personal development.

c. Building Empathy: Reflecting on our interactions fosters empathy. It allows us to step into others' shoes, understand their perspectives, and build stronger, more meaningful connections.

d. Navigating Conflicts: By reflecting on interpersonal conflicts, we learn about different viewpoints, our conflict resolution skills, and strategies to handle future disagreements constructively.

3.   The   Interplay: Self   and   Interactions
a. Personal Growth: The insights garnered from introspection and external interactions contribute to personal growth. They provide a holistic perspective, allowing for a more informed, comprehensive approach to life's challenges.

b.   Building   Authentic   Relationships: Genuine relationships stem from a deep understanding of oneself and others. Reflecting on our interactions and self helps in building authentic bonds based on trust, understanding, and mutual respect.

c. Influencing Change: As we reflect on ourselves and our interactions, we become more aware of the changes we wish to see in ourselves and in the world. This reflection drives us to take action, influence change, and make a positive impact.

d. Lifelong Learning: The cycle of self-reflection and understanding interactions ensures continuous learning. It pushes us to evolve, adapt, and grow throughout our lives.

Reflecting on oneself and interactions is akin to playing a harmonious symphony, where individual notes (self-reflection) blend seamlessly with a variety of instruments (interactions) to create a beautiful melody. It's about finding balance, learning continuously, and moving forward with a deeper understanding of oneself and the world. Engaging in this reflective practice paves the way for a richer, more fulfilling life, marked by personal growth, meaningful relationships, and a profound understanding of the human experience.

10.1 Keeping Ego in Check: "I'm much too much for that."

The statement "I'm much too much for that" is an intriguing encapsulation of the human ego. At a first glance, it could suggest self-worth or self-confidence, but upon deeper reflection, it potentially reveals the dangers of an inflated ego. The context of "Reflecting on Self and Interactions" lends itself to dissecting the role of ego in personal growth and relationships.

1. Understanding Ego:

The ego is our conscious mind, our sense of self-worth, and our identity. It's the voice in our head that distinguishes between the subjective and objective, between "I" and the "world." While a healthy ego is essential for self-assurance and motivation, an unchecked ego can spiral into narcissism, leading to overconfidence, arrogance, and a distorted sense of self-importance.

2. Self-Reflection and Ego:

The process of introspection allows individuals to understand their motivations, desires, and fears. It's during such introspective moments that one can confront the ego, identifying moments when it might be excessive or misdirected. "I'm much too much for that" can be a realization during self-reflection: recognizing when one's self-perception has grown larger than life and needs recalibration.

3. Ego in Interactions:

A ballooned ego can hinder genuine interactions. When one constantly feels "above" situations or people, it creates barriers. This attitude can lead to misunderstandings, missed opportunities for learning, and strained relationships. For instance, refusing to undertake a task or learn something new because "it's beneath me" can stifle growth.

4. Balancing Confidence and Humility:

While it's vital to recognize one's worth, it's equally important to temper it with humility. Statements like "I'm much too much for that" need introspection: Is it a genuine acknowledgment of one's capability, or is it a dismissal born from overestimation of oneself? A balance ensures that while we respect our worth, we remain open to learning, growth, and genuine connections.

5. Consequences of Unchecked Ego:

An unchecked ego can lead to several personal and professional setbacks:

- **Relational Strains**: Arrogance or the constant need to dominate can strain relationships. It can lead to conflicts and reduce collaborative synergies.
- **Missed Learning Opportunities**: An inflated ego can blind individuals to their areas of improvement, leading to missed opportunities for growth.

- **Increased Vulnerability**: Ironically, a massive ego makes individuals more vulnerable. The need to always "be right" or "be the best" can result in unnecessary pressures and mental health strains.

6. Strategies to Check the Ego:
- **Active Listening**: Paying genuine attention during interactions ensures that one is not always prioritizing their voice or opinion.
- **Feedback Acceptance**: Encouraging and accepting constructive feedback can be grounding.
- **Empathy**: Practicing empathy ensures understanding and valuing others' perspectives, curbing the ego's dominance.
- **Lifelong Learning**: Adopting a learner's mindset ensures that the individual remains open to growth, recognizing that there's always more to know.
-

7. The Power of Groundedness:
While the ego serves as a necessary part of our identity and confidence, groundedness is a formidable ally. Being grounded ensures that while one recognizes and celebrates their strengths, they remain connected to reality, respecting others, and acknowledging the vastness of what's yet to be known.

In conclusion, while the ego is a fundamental aspect of our psyche, guiding our sense of self-worth and confidence, it's imperative to ensure it remains a healthy, constructive force. "Reflecting on Self and Interactions" is not just an introspective exercise but a pathway to understanding, modulating, and optimizing the role of ego in our lives. It's about recognizing when we are "much too much" and finding the balance that promotes growth, harmony, and genuine connection.

The Tale of the Boastful Writer

In the heart of the city, where skyscrapers kissed the clouds and dreams took flight, there lived Julian, a writer of grand repute. His tales of adventure, love, and valor had enchanted countless readers. As the years rolled by and accolades poured in, Julian's bookshelves grew heavier, but so did his head.

At gatherings and soirees, Julian had developed a habit of flaunting his achievements, often beginning his sentences with, "In my best-seller," or "When I was awarded." He basked in the admiration showered upon him, believing he was unparalleled in his craft.

One evening, at a posh literary event, an eager young writer named Elara approached Julian. With sparkling eyes and a notebook full of dreams, she said, "Mr. Julian, I've admired your work for years. I've penned a short story and would be honored if you'd offer some critique."

Julian, without even glancing at the pages, replied with a smirk, "My dear, I'm much too much for that. Perhaps when you've achieved a fraction of my success, I might spare a moment." Elara's excitement faded, replaced by a mix of embarrassment and disappointment. She nodded quietly and retreated.

The evening wore on, and as fate would have it, the event organizers announced an impromptu storytelling challenge. The theme was humility. The hall buzzed with whispers and excitement. Julian, confident as ever, took the stage first.

But as he began to weave his tale, Julian found himself struggling. He had penned stories of heroes and adventures, of love and loss, but humility? It was a theme he had distanced himself from. His story meandered, lacking depth and connection. The applause at the end was polite but faint.

Elara, inspired by her earlier encounter, took the stage next. She spun a heartfelt tale of a mountain that believed it was the mightiest, only to realize that its true strength lay in nurturing the life that thrived on it. The hall echoed with genuine applause.

The evening ended, and Julian, once the star, now stood overshadowed by a novice. But this story isn't about his fall. It's about his rise.

The next morning, Elara found a note at her door. It read:

"Dear Elara,

Last night, I was reminded of a lesson I had long forgotten. My ego blinded me, but your story opened my eyes. I am sorry for my behavior. I'd be honored if you'd share your work with me.
Warm regards,
Julian."

From that day, Julian wasn't just known as a great writer but also a humble mentor. He often quoted, "Talents make us unique, but humility makes us human."

And so, in a city of towering dreams, the tale of the boastful writer became a lesson in humility, echoing the timeless truth that no matter how high we soar, our roots should remain grounded.

Lessons

From "The Tale of the Boastful Writer," several lessons can be gleaned:

1. **Humility Over Arrogance:** Success and accolades should not lead one to become arrogant. True greatness lies in remaining humble and grounded, regardless of one's achievements.
2. **Never Underestimate Others:** Every individual, regardless of their current status or experience, has the potential to offer something valuable. Dismissing someone based on perceived superiority can lead to missed opportunities.

3. **Ego is a Double-Edged Sword:** While confidence can drive one to achieve great heights, unchecked ego can also be one's downfall. It blinds one to their shortcomings and isolates them from genuine growth opportunities.
4. **Openness to Learning:** No matter how accomplished one might be, there's always something new to learn. Embracing a lifelong learner's mindset ensures continuous growth and evolution.
5. **Apologizing Shows Strength:** Recognizing one's mistakes and genuinely apologizing for them is a mark of true strength and character. It not only repairs relationships but also fosters respect.
6. **Inspiration Can Come from Unexpected Places:** Sometimes, the most profound lessons and inspirations come from places or individuals we least expect.
7. **Treat Others with Respect:** How one treats others, especially those seemingly 'below' them, is a true testament to their character. Kindness and respect should be universal, not conditional.
8. **Growth is Beyond Skill Alone:** Personal growth encompasses not just honing one's skills but also nurturing qualities like humility, empathy, and self-awareness.

10.2 Championing Healthy Dialogues: "I'd rather talk to people than about them."

In a world deeply entrenched in the allure of gossip and hearsay, the mantra "I'd rather talk to people than about them" emerges as a beacon of hope for fostering open communication and trust. This sentiment underscores the importance of direct dialogue and confrontation, over the more passive and often harmful act of talking behind someone's back.

When we choose to talk to people directly, we're prioritizing clarity and understanding. Discussing issues or even casual matters face-to-face or over direct communication channels minimizes the chances of misunderstandings. Indirect communication, on the other hand, often gets clouded by personal biases, interpretations, or even third-party opinions which may distort the original message.

Moreover, engaging in conversations about someone without their knowledge can perpetuate negative narratives, foster unnecessary conflicts, and damage trust. Such practices not only harm the individual being discussed but also the wider community or group, as it creates an atmosphere of suspicion and doubt. The person on the receiving end of such discussions may feel isolated, misunderstood, or betrayed when they eventually find out.

Choosing to speak directly with someone embodies respect for that individual. It's a nod to their autonomy, their right to explain, and to be part of the dialogue that concerns them. This approach also demonstrates a level of maturity and courage. It's not always easy to face someone and discuss sensitive topics, but it's a testament to the value one places on transparency and sincerity.

Additionally, talking directly to someone, especially in cases of conflicts or misunderstandings, offers an opportunity for growth for both parties. It's a chance to understand differing perspectives, rectify misconceptions, and even foster deeper connections. When we sideline assumptions and prioritize direct conversations, we often find that our shared human experiences are more common than we initially believed.

In a broader societal context, this philosophy encourages a culture of empathy and open-mindedness. Instead of pigeonholing individuals based on second-hand information or unchecked biases, we allow ourselves to be educated by the very individuals we're trying to understand. This leads to richer, more nuanced views on people and situations.

In essence, the principle of "I'd rather talk to people than about them" serves as a moral compass pointing towards a more understanding, cohesive, and authentic way of interacting. It encourages us to champion genuine interactions over superficial chatter, depth over breadth, and understanding over assumption.

Sophie's Gossip-free Resolution

Sophie always considered herself a good listener. At gatherings, friends would huddle around her, seeking solace and advice, drawn by her empathetic ear. But as is the nature of many close-knit communities, these conversations often veered into territories of gossip. For years, Sophie was the epicenter of stories — stories about people's lives, their choices, their secrets.

On a chilly winter evening, nestled in the warmth of a cozy café, Sophie's friend, Lila, whispered about Tom's failing marriage. "They say he's moved out," she shared, her voice a mix of concern and excitement. Sophie nodded, taking a sip of her cocoa, her mind wandering to Tom and the pain he must be enduring.

But then something happened that Sophie hadn't expected. As Lila delved deeper into the intricacies of Tom's personal life, an old schoolmate, Jenna, approached their table. Jenna, a woman known for her forthrightness, leaned in and said, "If you're so worried about Tom, maybe you should speak directly to him rather than discussing his life here."

The words hit Sophie hard. It wasn't a rebuke but a revelation.

That evening, Sophie sat by her window, gazing at the snowflakes gently caressing the ground. She pondered over Jenna's words. How many times had she engaged in such conversations, believing she was being supportive or simply "in the know"? How many times had she discussed someone's life without considering the weight and ramifications of her words?

With the dawn of the New Year, Sophie made a resolution. Not the usual ones like joining a gym or reading more books. It was deeper, more personal. She resolved to champion healthy dialogues. "I'd rather talk to people than about them," she vowed.

The transformation was beautiful yet challenging. Sophie started to change the direction of conversations that veered into gossip. She reached out to friends going through hardships, offering direct support rather than discussing their situations in hushed tones with others.

Soon, her reputation changed. She was no longer the epicenter of stories but a beacon of trust and genuine concern. Friends began to approach her, not with tidbits of information but with their hopes, fears, and dreams. Sophie became a harbor for heart-to-hearts.

The ripple effect of her resolution was felt in her circle. Conversations became richer, deeper, filled with understanding and empathy. They weren't just dialogues;

they were connections, bridges mending gaps, weaving the tapestry of genuine relationships.

Sophie's gossip-free resolution wasn't merely a New Year's pledge. It was a life-changing journey, a testament that the best conversations are those built on trust, respect, and love. And in the process, Sophie discovered the pure joy of truly listening, of understanding, and most importantly, of connecting.

Lessons

From Sophie's Gossip-free Resolution we can learn the following important lessons:

1. **The Power of Direct Communication:** It's always better to communicate directly with someone about their issues rather than discussing them with others. Direct conversation fosters understanding and minimizes misunderstandings.
2. **Gossip Undermines Trust:** Engaging in gossip can erode trust within a community or group of friends. When one becomes known as a gossip, it can strain or sever relationships, as people might hesitate to confide in them.
3. **The Ripple Effect of Actions:** One person's decision to change can influence and inspire others. Sophie's resolution shifted the dynamics of her entire circle, emphasizing the impact one individual can have on a larger group.

4. **Value of Genuine Relationships:** Authentic relationships are built on trust, understanding, and genuine concern. These qualities elevate conversations and connections beyond surface-level interactions.

5. **Self-reflection is Key:** It's crucial to periodically introspect and evaluate our behaviors and the consequences they have on others. Self-awareness can lead to transformative life decisions, as seen with Sophie's New Year resolution.

6. **The Role of Accountability:** When confronted with the truth about her behavior, Sophie took responsibility and decided to change. Accepting one's faults and actively working towards improvement is essential for personal growth.

7. **Quality Over Quantity in Conversations:** Deep, meaningful conversations that are filled with empathy and understanding are more fulfilling than numerous shallow talks. They form the backbone of strong relationships.

8. **The Joy of Genuine Listening:** Actively listening and being present in a conversation, without the intent to share or spread the information, can be a rewarding experience. It fosters deeper connections and mutual respect.

9. **The Impact of Third-party Perspectives:** Sometimes, it takes an outsider or a less involved party, like Jenna in the story, to provide clarity and a fresh perspective on our actions. Keeping an

open mind to such interventions can be enlightening.

10. **Personal Resolutions Can Be Life-changing:** New Year's resolutions or personal pledges don't always have to be about self-improvement in traditional senses, like fitness or learning. They can also be about interpersonal relationships and moral values, which can have profound effects on one's life and the lives of those around them.

Chapter 11: Choices, Support, and Growth

Every day, from the moment we wake up to when we go to sleep, we make choices. These can be as simple as what to wear or what to eat for breakfast. But sometimes, they're bigger, like deciding on a job, where to live, or whom to befriend.

Choices shape our lives. They reflect who we are, what we value, and where we want to go. Even deciding not to make a choice is, in itself, a choice. And while we might sometimes make wrong turns, every choice offers a lesson.

Life can be tough. It's like a journey with hills, valleys, and sometimes storms. This is where support comes in.

Support can be friends who listen when we're down, family who have our backs no matter what, or even kind strangers offering a helping hand. It's like having good shoes for a long walk. With the right support, our journey becomes a bit easier, and we feel less alone. It reminds us that we're part of a bigger community, and there's strength in unity.

Now, imagine you planted a seed in the ground. With sunlight, water, and time, it grows. Just like that seed, we humans also grow. But our growth is not just physical. It's also about learning, understanding, and evolving.

Every experience, good or bad, offers a chance to learn. Making a mistake might feel bad at the moment, but it's an opportunity to grow stronger and wiser. Just like muscles that need exercise to become strong, our character and wisdom grow when we face challenges.

As humans, our lives are a dance of choices, the rhythm of support, and the beauty of growth. By making informed choices, seeking support when needed, and embracing every chance to grow, we continue to evolve and journey forward on the path of life. It's a journey of becoming the best versions of ourselves.

11.1 Trusting One's Instincts: "I have no idea, so I'm doing this now."

Have you ever been in a situation where you feel a bit lost or unsure about what to do next? We all have. It's a common part of being human. Sometimes, we don't have all the answers, and that's okay.

The statement "I have no idea, so I'm doing this now" is all about trusting our gut feelings or instincts in such moments. Think of it like this: imagine you're at a crossroads and don't have a map. Instead of just standing there, feeling stuck, you decide to pick a road and start walking. Why? Because something inside you, your instinct, tells you it might be the right way.

Trusting our instincts is like having an inner compass. Even if we don't know exactly where we're headed, this compass can guide us. It's built from our past experiences, our feelings, and sometimes, just a hunch.

Why is this trust important for us as humans?
1. **Decisions Become Easier:** We face many choices every day. If we wait to have all the answers or for things to be perfect, we might never move. Trusting our instincts helps us make decisions faster.
2. **Boosts Confidence:** When we trust ourselves, we feel more confident. Even if we make a mistake, we learn from it and grow.
3. **Natural Survival Mechanism:** From the time we were cave people, our instincts have kept us safe from dangers. It's like a built-in alarm system.
4. **Fulfillment:** Sometimes, the best moments in life come from unexpected decisions made on a whim. These spontaneous choices can lead to adventures and memories.
5. **Learning:** Every choice, good or bad, teaches us something. If we trust our instincts and it doesn't work out, that's okay. We learn and get better for the next time.

So, the next time you're not sure about something, remember that it's okay to say, "I have no idea." But also remember to trust yourself, take a deep breath, and think, "I'm doing this now." Your instincts might just lead you to something amazing.

Lucas's Uncharted Adventure

Lucas was a planner. Every step, every decision, every aspect of his life was meticulously plotted on charts, spreadsheets, and to-do lists. The predictability of his world provided a comforting cocoon.

However, on his 30th birthday, he woke up with a peculiar sensation, a restlessness that his charts couldn't decipher. As he stared at the world map pinned on his wall, a wild thought crossed his mind: What if, just for once, he embarked on a journey without a plan?

With only a backpack, Lucas headed to the airport, buying a ticket to the first destination he pointed to with his eyes closed: Bali. Upon landing, without an itinerary, hotel booking, or even a basic understanding of the local language, Lucas felt a combination of exhilaration and fear.

He started his days with no clear plan. Often, he'd sit by the beach, letting the waves dictate his thoughts. Some days, he'd follow the inviting aroma of local cuisine, discovering hidden eateries and making friends with local chefs.

One day, while exploring the lush rice terraces, Lucas met Maya, a local guide. Seeing his intrigue yet clear lack of direction, she smiled and said, "You seem lost, but in a good way." Lucas laughed, admitting, "I have no idea, so I'm doing this now." Intrigued, Maya decided to show him around, not as a guide, but as a fellow adventurer.

They ventured into uncharted territories, ancient temples untouched by tourists, hidden waterfalls known only to locals, and caves holding centuries-old secrets. Maya taught Lucas the beauty of spontaneity, while Lucas shared his analytical perspective, helping her in her own journey of self-discovery.

Through their adventures, Lucas realized that while planning had its merits, there was an indescribable magic in letting go, in allowing instincts to take the lead. He learned to trust himself, his choices, and the journey itself.

When it was time to return, Lucas had no detailed charts or logs of his adventure. Instead, he had memories, stories, and a newfound belief in the power of instincts.

Back home, his friends were curious about his uncharacteristic trip. To which Lucas simply responded, "Sometimes, not having an idea is the best idea." And with that, he began integrating the magic of spontaneity into his well-planned life, proving that humans, despite their need for control, can thrive in the embrace of the unknown.

Lessons

From the story of "Lucas's Uncharted Adventure," we can extract several key lessons:

1. **Embrace the Unknown:** Life can be richer and more fulfilling when we step out of our comfort zones. Embracing the unfamiliar can lead to unexpected joys and discoveries.

2. **Trust Your Instincts:** While planning and strategy have their place, sometimes it's essential to trust our gut feelings and let them guide our actions.

3. **The Value of Spontaneity:** There's a unique joy in being spontaneous, letting go of predetermined plans, and allowing the journey to unfold naturally.

4. **Connection Beyond Boundaries:** No matter the differences in language, culture, or background, humans can connect deeply when they share experiences and open their minds to learn from one another.

5. **Balance is Key:** While Lucas learned the beauty of spontaneity, he didn't entirely discard his planning nature. The story suggests that a balanced approach to life, integrating both planning and spontaneity, can be most fulfilling.

6. **Personal Growth Through Exploration:** Stepping into the unknown and trusting one's instincts can lead to significant personal growth and self-awareness.

7. **Life Beyond Plans:** While plans provide a roadmap, life's most beautiful moments often happen off the beaten path, in the detours and unplanned adventures.

8. **Listening to Inner Desires:** Sometimes, the heart and soul yearn for experiences we might not logically understand. Listening to these inner nudges can lead to transformative experiences.

9. **The Power of Now:** The present moment, devoid of past regrets and future anxieties, holds immense potential. Embracing the "now" can be liberating.

10. **Re-evaluating Life's Approach:** Life has a way of teaching us lessons when we least expect them. Being open to re-evaluating our approach to life can pave the way for richer, more meaningful experiences.

In essence, Lucas's adventure reminds us that while structure and planning are valuable, there's immeasurable wealth in the unplanned, the unpredictable, and the instinctive moments of our lives.

11.2 Encouraging Strengths: "I don't want to support you in your weaknesses."

At first glance, this statement might come across as a bit harsh or unsupportive, but there's a deeper meaning. It's about fostering growth and encouraging people to tap into their strengths rather than becoming reliant on their weaknesses.

Imagine you have a friend who's incredibly talented at playing the guitar but is also a bit of a procrastinator. Every time he faces a minor challenge, he tends to give up, choosing instead to lounge around and watch TV. Now, if you were to just sit with him and watch TV every time he felt demotivated, you'd be supporting his weakness: his tendency to procrastinate. However, if you encourage him to push past his initial reluctance, remind him of his love for music, and motivate him to practice his guitar, you're supporting his strength.

Supporting strengths is about recognizing the best in people and helping them see it too. It's about reminding them of their abilities, passions, and potential. It's not about ignoring or neglecting their weaknesses but focusing more on what they excel at. When we constantly focus on weaknesses, it can be demotivating. It can make someone feel like they're not good enough or that their efforts are in vain.

On the other hand, focusing on strengths can boost confidence. When people are reminded of what they're good at, they feel empowered. They're more likely to take initiative, face challenges head-on, and push past their comfort zones.

It's also important to remember that everyone has their unique blend of strengths and weaknesses. What might be a strength for one person might be a weakness for another, and that's okay. The key is to recognize these individual strengths and foster an environment where they can flourish.

So, the next time you're faced with a situation where someone is leaning into their weakness, maybe try a different approach. Instead of indulging that weakness, remind them of their strengths, guide them back to what they're passionate about, and watch them thrive.

Ella's Tough Love Approach

Ella and Amy had been friends since childhood. They played together, studied together, and even dreamed together. But as they grew older, their paths began to diverge. Ella became a sports coach, passionate about helping people unlock their potential, while Amy began to drift, trying one hobby after another, never truly committing to anything.

One day, Amy approached Ella, looking for guidance. She had taken up painting, but within a few weeks, she wanted to give up. "It's just too hard," Amy sighed, hoping for Ella's usual comforting words.

Instead, Ella said, "Amy, I don't want to support you in your weaknesses. I want to help you discover and build on your strengths."

Amy was taken aback. This wasn't the Ella she knew. "What do you mean?" she asked, puzzled.

Ella took a deep breath. "Every time things get a little challenging, you give up. But I've seen you, Amy. When you truly love something, you shine. Do you remember when you used to make those handcrafted cards? The joy in your eyes, the hours you'd spend perfecting each design? That's your strength. That's where your passion lies."

Amy thought back and remembered those days. She did love making cards. But over time, she had forgotten about it, always chasing something new, something different.

Ella continued, "Instead of jumping from one thing to another, focus on what you truly love. Dive deep into it. Yes, it'll be tough, and there will be challenges. But remember, I'll be here, cheering for you, supporting you in your strengths."

Inspired by Ella's words, Amy rekindled her passion for card-making. She began attending workshops, refining her skills, and soon started her own small business. The cards she crafted weren't just pieces of paper; they were embodiments of love, joy, and memories.

Ella's tough love approach was just the push Amy needed. She learned the value of commitment and the joy that comes from truly immersing oneself in their passion.

Their friendship stood the test of time, a testament to the power of true support. For in Ella's wisdom, Amy found her path, and together, they proved that sometimes, the best way to help someone is not by cushioning their falls, but by guiding them to stand tall and chase their dreams.

Lessons

From "Ella's Tough Love Approach," we can derive several key lessons:

1. **Recognizing True Passion:** It's crucial to differentiate between fleeting interests and genuine passions. While it's okay to explore, it's equally essential to recognize and invest in what truly resonates with one's heart.

2. **Consistency Over Temporary Efforts:** Jumping from one hobby to another might seem exciting, but true mastery and fulfillment often come from consistent effort in one direction.

3. **The Value of Tough Love:** Sometimes, the best way to support someone is not by endorsing their every move, but by challenging them to face their weaknesses and work on their strengths.

4. **The Role of Genuine Friends:** True friends are not just there during easy times but will also guide, advise, and sometimes provide the necessary push during challenging periods.

5. **Strength in Persistence:** When faced with challenges, persistence and determination can lead to unexpected rewards. Giving up at the first sign of difficulty denies one the opportunity to grow and excel.

6. **Rediscovery of Lost Passions:** It's never too late to return to a forgotten passion or hobby. Past

interests can serve as a foundation for future endeavors.

7. **Support in Strengths, Not Weaknesses:** By focusing on and nurturing someone's strengths rather than their weaknesses, we empower them to be their best selves.

8. **Commitment Leads to Growth:** Committing to a particular path or passion can lead to personal and professional growth, as seen with Amy's successful card-making business.

9. **Listening to Constructive Feedback:** Instead of getting defensive or disheartened by constructive criticism, embracing it can pave the way for personal development.

10. **Value of Self-awareness:** Recognizing one's patterns, like Amy's tendency to give up when faced with challenges, is the first step towards change and growth.

Chapter 12: Concluding with Trust and Calm

Let's think about "trust" first. Trust is a foundational element in any relationship, be it personal or professional. When we trust, we're essentially believing in the reliability, truth, or ability of someone or something. It's like giving someone an invisible thread that connects both of you. This thread is delicate, and once broken, it's hard to mend. By concluding interactions with trust, it means ending on a note where both parties feel confident in the bond they share, and they believe in each other's intentions and actions.

Now, "calm." In many ways, calmness is a state of peace and tranquility. It's the opposite of agitation or excitement. It's like a still lake, undisturbed by wind or rain. When we conclude with calm, we're ensuring that any interaction or situation we're a part of ends without any lingering anxieties, doubts, or unrest. This could be as simple as resolving an argument without anger, or as complex as making a challenging life decision with clarity and peace.

When we combine trust and calm, we're basically ensuring that we wrap up any situation, conversation, or interaction in a way that leaves everyone involved feeling secure and at peace. This approach is valuable because, in life, it's not just about the journey but also how we end it. Concluding with trust and calm ensures that we're leaving things on a positive note, setting the stage for future interactions and situations to start on the right foot.

Imagine a world where everyone embraced this idea! We'd have fewer misunderstandings, deeper relationships, and more collective peace of mind.

12.1 The Grace of Belief: "Fine, then I'll take your word for it."

This captures a fundamental essence of human interaction, which is trust. In the context of concluding with trust and calm, this phrase embodies the decision to place faith in someone else's words or actions without allowing skepticism to cloud judgment.

Imagine you're having a discussion with a friend about a recent event you didn't witness. You have your doubts based on what you've heard or perceived, but your friend shares a different perspective. Now, you're at a crossroads. You could choose to delve deeper, question more, or even dispute their version. But, sometimes, it's more peaceful and affirming to simply say, "Fine, then I'll take your word for it."

This decision to believe doesn't mean you're naive or that you accept everything at face value. Rather, it reflects an understanding that endless questioning or skepticism can be exhausting and counterproductive. It's about picking battles wisely and recognizing that, sometimes, peace and mutual respect are more valuable than being right or knowing every detail.

Relating it to "Concluding with Trust and Calm," the idea is to finish interactions on a note of trust. Conclusions mark endings, and when we conclude with trust, we lay a foundation for future interactions to be built on mutual respect and understanding. It's about leaving the door open for faith, for believing in the goodness of others, and for fostering a calm environment where people feel heard and validated.

Furthermore, taking someone at their word is a reflection of your character as much as theirs. It shows that you value the relationship enough to place trust in it. This grace of belief can also have a calming effect on you. Instead of ruminating over details or inconsistencies, you choose to find tranquility in trust.

So, in essence, the statement "Fine, then I'll take your word for it" is more than just passive acceptance. It's a conscious choice to prioritize peace, trust, and the well-being of a relationship over doubts and disputes.

The Legend of the Trusting Village

Once upon a time, nestled between rolling hills and deep valleys, lay the village of Veritas. The people of Veritas were known far and wide for one unique trait: their unwavering trust in each other.

It all began generations ago when the founder of Veritas, Old Man Cedric, laid down a single rule for his village: "In Veritas, we take each other at their word." This rule was etched onto the village entrance and was the first thing visitors would see upon arrival.

In the heart of Veritas stood the Great Oak. Legend had it that every promise made under its sprawling branches was bound to be true. It was here that villagers would come to make important declarations, strike deals, or resolve disputes.

One day, a cunning merchant named Gilbert arrived in Veritas. Seeing the trust that the villagers had in each other, he hatched a plan to take advantage of them. He set up a stall beneath the Great Oak, selling what he claimed to be 'magic beans' that could heal any ailment.

The village healer, a wise old woman named Mira, was skeptical. She approached the merchant, "Are these beans truly magical as you claim?"

Without hesitation, Gilbert responded, "Of course! Believe me, they work wonders!"

Mira, looking deep into his eyes, remembered the principle of Veritas and said, "Fine, then I'll take your word for it." She decided to buy a bean, but instead of using it, she planted it beside her home.

Weeks passed, and to Gilbert's surprise and Mira's anticipation, a robust beanstalk grew from where the bean was sown. However, there was no magic to be seen. The villagers who had bought the beans came to realize that they held no special power.

Feeling guilty for misleading the villagers, Gilbert approached Mira, "I am sorry for lying. I never expected the bean to grow and reveal my deceit."

Mira, with a gentle smile, replied, "In Veritas, we believe in giving trust freely. But remember, trust once broken is hard to mend."

Realizing the weight of his actions, Gilbert decided to stay in Veritas and work alongside the villagers, learning the true value of trust and honesty. The beanstalk served as a reminder of the grace of belief and the responsibility that came with it.

And so, the legend of the trusting village grew, teaching generations the simple yet profound lesson: While it's a gift to trust openly, it's an honor to be truly trustworthy.

Lessons

From "The Legend of the Trusting Village," we can derive several key lessons:

1. **The Power of Trust:** A community built on trust can thrive. The villagers of Veritas were united and harmonious because of their unwavering belief in each other.
2. **Trust Can Be Misused:** Just because a community or individual is trusting does not mean they are

immune to deception. Gilbert saw the villagers' trust as an opportunity for exploitation.

3. **Responsibility of Trust:** When trust is freely given, as with Mira believing Gilbert, there's an inherent responsibility for the trusted party not to betray that confidence.

4. **Actions Reveal the Truth:** Mira's act of planting the bean instead of using it highlighted that actions, over time, can reveal the truth behind words and promises.

5. **Trust, Once Broken, is Hard to Mend:** While the villagers were trusting, the betrayal of their trust wasn't without consequences. It serves as a reminder that while trust can be given freely, rebuilding it once lost is a challenging task.

6. **Integrity Over Deception:** Gilbert's realization of his wrongdoing and decision to stay and integrate into the community of Veritas emphasized the importance of honesty and integrity over short-term gains from deception.

7. **Symbols Carry Weight:** The beanstalk, growing tall and robust, served as a constant reminder of both the grace of trust and the repercussions of deceit.

8. **The Grace of Second Chances:** Even after being deceived, the villagers gave Gilbert a chance to redeem himself, showcasing the strength of forgiveness and the possibility of redemption.

9. **Honesty is an Honor:** Being trustworthy isn't just a responsibility; it's an honor. In a trusting

community, those who maintain their honesty are held in the highest regard.

10. **Foundational Values Shape Communities:** Old Man Cedric's foundational rule for Veritas shaped the community's ethos for generations, emphasizing the lasting impact of core values on societies.

12.2 The Art of Slow Living: "Then I'd rather take it easy."

In today's world, it feels like everything is moving at a breakneck speed. Technology, jobs, even our daily routines seem to be on a never-ending sprint. Amidst this rush, there's a growing movement, an art really, called slow living. It's about choosing to take things easy instead of always being on the go.

Imagine you're watching a movie and you press the 'pause' button. Everything stops, right? Slow living is a bit like that. It's about pressing 'pause' on our lives, even if just for a little while, to enjoy the moment. It doesn't mean being lazy or not doing anything. It's more about choosing to do things at a pace where you can really appreciate them.

Let's take cooking as an example. Instead of quickly throwing together a meal or ordering fast food, slow living encourages us to take our time. Maybe we'll choose fresh ingredients, enjoy the process of preparing them, and relish the meal with family or friends. It's about savoring every bite, every moment.

Now, think about conversations. Have you ever chatted with someone and realized neither of you is truly listening? Slow living means taking the time to genuinely listen and understand what the other person is saying. It's about being present in the conversation.

But why is slow living becoming so popular? Well, constantly racing against the clock can be stressful. We're always thinking about the next thing, the next task, and we forget to enjoy what we're doing right now. Slow living helps us find balance. It reminds us that it's okay to take a step back, to relax, and to enjoy life's simple pleasures.

Imagine reading a book without skimming through the pages or walking in a park without rushing to get to the end. It's these moments, these breaks, that can make us feel happier and more connected to the world around us.

In conclusion, the art of slow living is about choosing to take it easy, to relish in the present, and to connect more deeply with our experiences. It's an invitation to enjoy life's journey, rather than just hurrying to the destination.

Milo's Day Off

Milo was always in a hurry. Every morning, the alarm clock would scream at 6 am, and he'd rush out the door, grabbing a quick toast and coffee, to start his long day. Meetings, reports, deadlines - life was a constant race against the clock.

But one Wednesday, something unusual happened. Milo woke up without the shrill cry of the alarm. The sun was already high, its gentle rays filtering through the curtains. Puzzled, he checked the time. It was 9 am. He had overslept!

His first instinct was to panic. There were emails to answer, tasks to complete! But as he began to hustle, he caught a glimpse of the world outside. Birds chirped, trees swayed gently, and the neighborhood kids played on their bikes, laughing and shouting. It was a simple, serene sight, but one Milo rarely noticed.

A thought struck him, "Why not take a day off? Just one day." With a hint of rebellion, he switched off his phone, resisting the pull of work and responsibilities. "Then I'd rather take it easy," he murmured to himself.

Milo decided to do everything he usually didn't have time for. He made a leisurely breakfast, with pancakes, fresh fruits, and a cup of slow-brewed coffee. He took a walk in the park, feeling the grass beneath his feet and listening to the rhythmic croak of the frogs in the pond. He even sat on a bench, closing his eyes, feeling the sun on his face, and just...breathing.

Lunch was at a small café nearby. He didn't grab a sandwich and rush out. Instead, he savored each bite, chatted with the café owner, and even made a new friend - a retired teacher who introduced him to the joys of bird-watching.

The day passed with Milo reading a book, taking a short nap, and even trying his hand at cooking dinner. No TV, no screens. Just Milo, his thoughts, and the simple pleasures of life.

As the day came to an end, Milo realized he felt more refreshed than he had in years. He had reconnected with himself, found joy in the mundane, and understood the art of slow living.

From that day on, Milo changed. While he couldn't always take the day off, he made sure to take out moments from his busy life to breathe, to live slowly, and to cherish the world around him. Because sometimes, the best way to move forward is by taking a step back and taking it easy.

Lessons

From "Milo's Day Off," we can draw several key lessons:

1. **Importance of Pausing:** No matter how busy life gets, it's essential to occasionally hit the 'pause' button. Taking time for oneself can provide much-needed refreshment and clarity.

2. **Rediscovering Simple Pleasures:** Often, in the hustle and bustle of daily life, we overlook the simple joys around us, like the chirping of birds or the laughter of children. Reconnecting with these moments can offer profound happiness.

3. **Disconnect to Connect:** Switching off digital devices, even if just for a day, can help us reconnect with ourselves, our environment, and the people around us.

4. **Quality Over Quantity:** A day spent doing fewer, more meaningful activities can be more rewarding than a week filled with rushed, unfulfilling tasks.
5. **The Value of the Present:** Living in the moment, or practicing mindfulness, can lead to a deeper appreciation for life as it unfolds.
6. **Embracing Slow Living:** In a world obsessed with speed, there's a unique beauty in taking things slow. Slow living allows for richer experiences and a deeper connection with our surroundings.
7. **Flexibility in Routine:** While routines provide structure, it's equally important to be flexible and allow spontaneous moments to shape our days.
8. **Recharging is Essential:** Just like how electronics need recharging, so do humans. A day off or even a few hours of self-care can rejuvenate the mind and body.
9. **Nature as a Healer:** Spending time in nature, even if it's just a city park, can have therapeutic effects on our well-being.
10. **Relationships and Community:** Interacting with those around us, like neighbors or local business owners, can foster a sense of community and belonging. Even brief, genuine interactions can leave a lasting impact.

In essence, "Milo's Day Off" reminds us that amidst life's chaos, there's profound wisdom in slowing down, savoring the present, and cherishing the simple joys that life offers.

Conclusion: The Lasting Impact of Words and Stories in Shaping Our Lives

In our ceaseless quest to navigate the multifaceted realm of existence, we often underestimate the silent power woven into the fabric of words and the tales they tell. The stories shared throughout this book, rooted in 25 transformative sentences, spotlight the profound influence that simple expressions can wield upon our lives.

Every phrase we've delved into, from the assertion of personal boundaries with "I'd rather talk to people than about them," to the embrace of slow living in "Then I'd rather take it easy," underscores a universal truth: Words are not just mere combinations of letters. They are carriers of emotions, harbingers of change, and instruments of revelation. They define our realities, mold our perceptions, and most significantly, steer the course of our actions.

The tales of Maria's sacrifices, James' unsent letter, and Milo's Day off aren't just narratives; they are reflections of shared human experiences. They remind us that life, in its boundless diversity, is a mosaic of choices, emotions, and moments. Embracing these moments, making conscious choices, and understanding our emotions all pivot on the axis of effective communication with ourselves and others.

The story of Sophie, for instance, emphasizes the gravitas of speaking directly to individuals rather than about them. Such straightforward, honest dialogues nurture trust and cultivate environments where authenticity thrives. Similarly, the narrative of Alice's U-turn decision throws light on the beauty of adaptability and the significance of being open to change, demonstrating that our decisions are but transient moments in the grand journey of life.

The variety of stories presented, each tethered to a simple yet profound sentence, serves as a testament to the universality of human experiences. Irrespective of our backgrounds, cultures, or life paths, we're all united in our search for understanding, meaning, and connection. And often, it is through words and stories that we find them.

In conclusion, while life's complex dance unfolds in countless ways, the essence of our journey often boils down to the words we choose and the stories we tell and listen to. They are our compass, our solace, our bridge to others, and most crucially, our mirror to introspect. By recognizing and valuing the impact of these 25 sentences, we are not just simplifying life but also enriching it, guiding ourselves and others towards understanding, empathy, and fulfillment.